Navigating Unrealistic Budget Expectations: A Guide for New Entrepreneurs

Priscilla Rogers and Ishan Khan

Published by Priscilla Rogers, 2024.

While every precaution has been taken in the preparation of this book, the publisher assumes no responsibility for errors or omissions, or for damages resulting from the use of the information contained herein.

NAVIGATING UNREALISTIC BUDGET EXPECTATIONS: A GUIDE FOR NEW ENTREPRENEURS

First edition. February 25, 2024.

Copyright © 2024 Priscilla Rogers and Ishan Khan.

ISBN: 979-8224005628

Written by Priscilla Rogers and Ishan Khan.

Also by Priscilla Rogers

Living Right - Moral Stories For A Beautiful Life
Living Right - 50 Stories Of Moral Clarity - Book 1
Living Right - 50 Stories Of Moral Clarity - Book 2
Living Right - 50 Stories Of Moral Clarity - Book 3

Standalone
Christmas Stories of Joy - 50 Short Stories
Flash of Fantasy - 50 Magical Adventures
Flashback: 50 Stories of Nostalgia
Love In A Flash - 50 Romantic Short Stories
Uptown, Downtown, All Around: New York Short Stories.
Stoicism Unbound: Navigating the Modern World with Ancient Wisdom
Sweet Dreams Delight: 30 Bedtime Short Stories
Navigating Unrealistic Budget Expectations: A Guide for New Entrepreneurs

Also by Ishan Khan

Flash Frights: 50 Terrifying Tales of Horror
Flash of Fantasy - 50 Magical Adventures
Flashback: 50 Stories of Nostalgia
Sci-Fi Snapshots: 50 Quick Trips To The Future
Whispers In The Dark - 50 Short Thriller Stories
Uptown, Downtown, All Around: New York Short Stories.
Mumbai: City of Dreams, Stories of Reality.
Secrets And Shadows: 25 Short Thriller Stories.
Navigating Unrealistic Budget Expectations: A Guide for New Entrepreneurs

Table of Contents

1. Understanding Unrealistic Budget Expectations.

———

Welcome to Chapter 1 of our book, where we embark on a journey to unravel the complexities of dealing with unrealistic budget expectations from clients. In this chapter, we delve into the fundamental concepts surrounding unrealistic budget expectations, shedding light on what they entail, why they occur, and the profound impact they can have on entrepreneurial ventures.

As entrepreneurs and freelancers, navigating the delicate balance between client expectations and financial feasibility is a constant challenge. Unrealistic budget expectations present a particularly daunting hurdle, often leaving service providers grappling with the dilemma of delivering quality work within constrained budgets.

To effectively tackle this challenge, it's essential to first understand what constitutes unrealistic budget expectations. In this chapter, we'll define the term, explore its various manifestations, and examine the underlying factors that contribute to its emergence. By gaining a deeper understanding of this concept, entrepreneurs can equip themselves with the knowledge and insights needed to navigate client interactions with confidence and clarity.

Join us as we embark on this exploration of understanding unrealistic budget expectations, laying the groundwork for subsequent chapters where we'll delve into communication strategies, negotiation tactics, and practical tips for managing client expectations effectively.

∧∧∧∧

i. Defining Unrealistic Budget Expectations.

In the realm of business, particularly for entrepreneurs and freelancers, the term "unrealistic budget expectations" encapsulates a common challenge: clients expecting more than what their allocated budget realistically permits. It's a nuanced concept that touches upon the delicate balance between clients' desires, financial constraints, and the feasibility of delivering high-quality work within those parameters.

At its core, unrealistic budget expectations refer to the scenario where clients demand an extensive array of services, features, or deliverables while offering a budget that doesn't align with the scope or complexity of the project. In other words, it's the dissonance between what clients envision and what is financially viable for the entrepreneur or service provider.

Consider this scenario: a client approaches a freelance web designer with a request for a custom-designed website with intricate features, e-commerce functionality, and a tight deadline. However, the client's budget is a fraction of what it would typically cost to develop such a complex website. In this scenario, the client's expectations regarding the breadth and depth of the project far exceed what their budget allows, thus constituting unrealistic budget expectations.

Unrealistic budget expectations can manifest in various forms, each presenting its unique challenges. Some clients may underestimate the time and effort required to complete a project, leading them to offer a budget that falls short of covering the necessary resources. Others may have inflated expectations fueled by a misunderstanding of industry standards or the perceived value of the services being provided.

One of the key indicators of unrealistic budget expectations is the discrepancy between the scope of work outlined by the client and the resources (time, expertise, materials) required to fulfill those requirements. Clients may demand extensive revisions, additional features, or expedited timelines without considering the financial implications for the service provider.

Moreover, unrealistic budget expectations can arise when clients fail to grasp the intricacies and complexities involved in delivering certain services or projects. For instance, a client may request a comprehensive marketing campaign without fully understanding the costs associated with market research, content creation, advertising, and analytics tracking.

The consequences of unrealistic budget expectations can be far-reaching, impacting both the client and the service provider. For clients, unrealistic expectations can result in dissatisfaction with the final deliverables, as they may not meet the standards or specifications initially outlined. This dissatisfaction can strain the client-provider relationship and tarnish the reputation of both parties involved.

From the perspective of the service provider, unrealistic budget expectations pose significant challenges to profitability, resource allocation, and overall business sustainability. Spending excessive time and resources on projects with inadequate budgets can lead to financial losses and hinder the ability to take on more lucrative opportunities.

Factors contributing to unrealistic budget expectations are multifaceted and often rooted in clients' past experiences, industry norms, and perceptions of value. Clients may draw upon previous engagements where they received a higher level of service for a lower cost, leading them to expect similar treatment in future interactions. Additionally, misconceptions about the standard rates or pricing structures within a particular industry can contribute to unrealistic expectations regarding budget.

It's important to recognize that unrealistic budget expectations are not solely the result of clients being unreasonable or demanding. Rather, they often stem from a lack of clarity, communication, or education regarding the intricacies of the project and the associated costs.

In conclusion, defining unrealistic budget expectations involves recognizing the misalignment between clients' desired outcomes and the financial constraints within which those outcomes must be achieved. By understanding the nuances of this concept, entrepreneurs can better navigate client interactions, set realistic expectations, and foster mutually beneficial relationships built on transparency and trust.

^^^^

ii. The Psychology Behind Clients' Budget Expectations.

Understanding the psychology behind clients' budget expectations is essential for entrepreneurs and freelancers striving to navigate the intricacies of client interactions successfully. Clients' perceptions, past experiences, and underlying motivations all play a pivotal role in shaping their expectations regarding budget. By delving into the psychological factors at play, service providers can gain valuable insights that inform their communication strategies, negotiation tactics, and overall approach to managing client expectations.

1. Past Experiences:

Clients' past experiences with service providers significantly influence their expectations regarding budget. Positive experiences, where clients received high-quality work within their budgetary constraints, may lead them to expect similar outcomes in future engagements. Conversely, negative experiences, such as projects exceeding budget or failing to meet expectations, can make clients more cautious and skeptical when setting budgetary parameters for new projects.

Moreover, past experiences with specific industries or service providers can shape clients' perceptions of what constitutes a reasonable budget. For example, clients accustomed to working with providers who offer discounted rates or bundle services may expect similar pricing structures from other providers, even if their services differ in scope or quality.

Understanding clients' past experiences allows service providers to tailor their approach to meet clients where they are, addressing any concerns or preconceptions that may influence their budget expectations. By acknowledging and empathizing with clients' past experiences, service providers can build trust and rapport, laying the groundwork for productive and mutually beneficial collaborations.

2. Perceived Value:

Clients' perceptions of the value they receive for their investment significantly influence their budget expectations. Perceived value encompasses not only the tangible deliverables or outcomes of a project but also the intangible benefits, such as expertise, reliability, and customer service, that clients associate with a service provider.

Clients are more likely to accept higher budgets when they perceive the value of the services being provided to outweigh the costs. Conversely, when clients perceive a disconnect between the proposed budget and the anticipated value of the project, they may push back or seek alternative solutions that better align with their expectations.

Service providers can enhance perceived value by clearly articulating the benefits and outcomes clients can expect from their services. This may involve highlighting past successes, showcasing testimonials or case studies, and demonstrating expertise in relevant areas. By effectively communicating the value proposition of their services, service providers can justify higher budgets and alleviate concerns about perceived discrepancies between cost and value.

3. Social Comparisons:

Clients often engage in social comparisons when assessing the fairness and reasonableness of budget expectations. Social comparisons involve comparing one's own situation or circumstances to those of others, particularly peers or competitors, to gauge whether their expectations are in line with prevailing norms or standards.

For example, a client may compare the budget proposed by a service provider to budgets offered by other providers in the same industry or to budgets allocated for similar projects within their organization. If the proposed budget deviates significantly from these benchmarks, clients may question its fairness or reasonableness, leading to friction or dissatisfaction.

Service providers can mitigate the impact of social comparisons by providing context and justification for their proposed budgets. This may involve explaining the unique value proposition of their services, highlighting the expertise or resources they bring to the table, and demonstrating how their proposed budget aligns with industry standards or best practices.

4. Risk Perception:

Clients' perception of risk also influences their budget expectations, particularly regarding the potential for cost overruns, delays, or unforeseen challenges. Clients may be more inclined to accept higher budgets if they perceive the project as low-risk, with minimal potential for disruptions or setbacks.

Conversely, clients may be more cautious and conservative when setting budgets for projects perceived as high-risk or uncertain. In such cases, clients may seek to mitigate risk by imposing stricter budgetary constraints or requiring additional assurances from the service provider.

Service providers can address clients' risk perceptions by proactively identifying and mitigating potential risks associated with the project. This may involve conducting thorough risk assessments, developing contingency plans, and providing transparent communication throughout the project lifecycle. By instilling confidence in their ability to manage risks effectively, service providers can alleviate clients' concerns and build trust, facilitating smoother negotiations and agreement on budgetary parameters.

In conclusion, the psychology behind clients' budget expectations is multifaceted, encompassing past experiences, perceived value, social comparisons, and risk perceptions. By understanding these psychological factors, service providers can tailor their approach to effectively manage client expectations, navigate negotiations, and ultimately, cultivate successful and mutually beneficial collaborations. By acknowledging and addressing clients' underlying motivations and concerns, service providers can build trust, enhance perceived value, and lay the foundation for long-term client relationships built on mutual respect and understanding.

∧∧∧∧

iii. Impact Of Unrealistic Budgets On Business Operations And Profitability.

Unrealistic budgets can have far-reaching consequences for businesses, affecting various aspects of operations, profitability, and overall sustainability. In this section, we'll delve into the profound impact that unrealistic budgets can have on business operations and profitability, highlighting the challenges they pose and strategies for mitigating their adverse effects.

1. Underestimation of Costs:

One of the most immediate impacts of unrealistic budgets is the underestimation of project costs. When clients demand extensive services or deliverables within a limited budget, service providers may be forced to compromise on quality, cut corners, or allocate insufficient resources to meet project requirements adequately. This underestimation of costs can lead to financial strain, as service providers may find themselves unable to cover expenses or allocate resources effectively.

2. Overcommitment of Resources:

Unrealistic budgets can also result in the overcommitment of resources, as service providers attempt to fulfill client demands within constrained budgets. This overcommitment may manifest in the form of allocating excessive time, manpower, or other resources to projects with inadequate budgets, thereby diverting resources away from more profitable opportunities. Over time, this can lead to burnout, inefficiencies, and diminished productivity within the organization.

3. Compromised Quality:

In an effort to adhere to unrealistic budgets, service providers may be tempted to compromise on the quality of their work. This could involve cutting corners, rushing through tasks, or using subpar materials or resources to meet client expectations within budgetary constraints. However, compromising on quality not only undermines the value proposition of the service provider but also jeopardizes client satisfaction and long-term relationships. Clients may ultimately be dissatisfied with the final deliverables, leading to reputational damage and loss of future business.

4. Financial Losses:

Perhaps the most significant impact of unrealistic budgets is the potential for financial losses. When projects exceed budgetary constraints or fail to generate sufficient revenue to cover costs, service providers may incur financial losses that impact their bottom line. These losses can erode profitability, strain cash flow, and hinder the ability to invest in growth opportunities or sustain operations over the long term. Moreover, financial losses resulting from unrealistic budgets can have cascading effects, impacting employee morale, stakeholder confidence, and overall organizational resilience.

5. Opportunity Costs:

Unrealistic budgets can also result in opportunity costs, as service providers may forego more lucrative opportunities in favor of projects with inadequate budgets. By allocating resources to projects that fail to generate sufficient returns, service providers miss out on the opportunity to pursue higher-value projects that could contribute significantly to their bottom line. Over time, this can hinder growth, limit expansion opportunities, and compromise the competitiveness of the business in the marketplace.

Mitigating the Impact:

While the impact of unrealistic budgets on business operations and profitability can be significant, there are strategies that service providers can employ to mitigate their adverse effects:

Transparent Communication: Foster open and transparent communication with clients regarding budget constraints, project scope, and resource requirements. Set realistic expectations from the outset and proactively address any discrepancies or concerns that may arise.

Value-Based Pricing: Shift the focus from cost to value by implementing value-based pricing strategies that emphasize the unique benefits and outcomes clients can expect from your services. Educate clients on the value proposition of your offerings and how they justify the proposed budget.

Scope Management: Implement robust scope management processes to prevent scope creep and ensure that projects remain within budgetary constraints. Clearly define project scope, deliverables, and milestones, and communicate any deviations or changes that may impact budgetary parameters.

Strategic Partnerships: Forge strategic partnerships with vendors, suppliers, and other service providers to leverage economies of scale, reduce costs, and enhance operational efficiency. Collaborate with partners who share your commitment to quality and client satisfaction, thereby extending your capabilities without compromising on standards.

Continuous Improvement: Continuously evaluate and refine your business processes, systems, and practices to optimize efficiency, reduce waste, and maximize profitability. Embrace a culture of continuous improvement and innovation, seeking feedback from clients, employees, and stakeholders to identify areas for enhancement.

In conclusion, the impact of unrealistic budgets on business operations and profitability cannot be overstated. From underestimation of costs to compromised quality and financial losses, unrealistic budgets pose significant challenges for service providers striving to meet client expectations while maintaining profitability. However, by adopting proactive communication strategies, implementing value-based pricing, and fostering a culture of continuous improvement, service providers can mitigate the adverse effects of unrealistic budgets and position themselves for long-term success and sustainability.

2. Communicating Effectively.

Welcome to Chapter 2 of our book, where we delve into the importance of effective communication in navigating unrealistic budget expectations from clients. Effective communication lies at the heart of successful client relationships, serving as a cornerstone for establishing trust, managing expectations, and finding mutually beneficial solutions.

In this chapter, we explore the essential elements of effective communication when dealing with unrealistic budget expectations. From setting clear boundaries to fostering open dialogue and active listening, effective communication techniques are indispensable tools for entrepreneurs and freelancers striving to navigate challenging client interactions with confidence and clarity.

Join us as we embark on this exploration of effective communication strategies, equipping you with the skills and insights needed to navigate negotiations, address concerns, and build strong, lasting relationships with your clients. Through proactive and transparent communication, you can mitigate misunderstandings, align expectations, and ultimately, deliver value within budgetary constraints.

∧∧∧∧

i. Importance Of Clear And Transparent Communication.

Clear and transparent communication is the cornerstone of successful client relationships, particularly when dealing with unrealistic budget expectations. In this section, we'll explore the importance of clear and transparent communication in navigating budgetary constraints, fostering trust, and achieving mutually satisfactory outcomes.

1. Establishing Trust:

Clear and transparent communication is essential for establishing trust between service providers and clients. When clients feel informed and involved in the decision-making process, they are more likely to trust the expertise and integrity of the service provider. Conversely, a lack of transparency can breed skepticism and erode trust, leading to strained relationships and dissatisfaction.

By proactively communicating with clients about budgetary constraints, project scope, and potential challenges, service providers demonstrate their commitment to honesty, integrity, and accountability. This transparency fosters trust and confidence, laying the foundation for productive and collaborative partnerships built on mutual respect and understanding.

2. Managing Expectations:

Effective communication is instrumental in managing client expectations, particularly when it comes to budgetary constraints. By clearly articulating what can and cannot be achieved within the allocated budget, service providers help clients set realistic expectations and avoid potential disappointments or misunderstandings down the line.

Transparent communication also enables service providers to address any misconceptions or unrealistic assumptions that clients may have regarding project scope, deliverables, or timelines. By openly discussing the limitations and challenges associated with the project, service providers empower clients to make informed decisions and adjust their expectations accordingly.

3. Aligning Objectives:

Clear and transparent communication facilitates the alignment of objectives between service providers and clients. By openly discussing project goals, priorities, and desired outcomes, both parties can ensure that their expectations are aligned and that they are working towards a shared vision of success.

When it comes to budgetary constraints, transparent communication enables service providers to explain the rationale behind their proposed budget and how it aligns with the client's objectives and priorities. By highlighting the value proposition of their services and the potential benefits of investing in quality work, service providers can garner buy-in from clients and secure their commitment to the proposed budget.

4. Building Rapport:

Effective communication is instrumental in building rapport and fostering positive relationships with clients. By demonstrating empathy, active listening, and responsiveness, service providers show that they value their clients' input and are committed to meeting their needs and expectations.

Transparent communication also creates opportunities for open dialogue and feedback, allowing clients to express their concerns, ask questions, and provide input throughout the project lifecycle. By actively engaging with clients and soliciting their feedback, service providers can strengthen the client-provider relationship and foster a sense of partnership and collaboration.

5. Resolving Conflicts:

Clear and transparent communication is essential for resolving conflicts and addressing challenges that may arise during the project. When conflicts arise over budgetary constraints or other issues, open and honest communication enables both parties to express their concerns, identify potential solutions, and work towards a resolution.

By approaching conflicts with empathy, respect, and a willingness to listen, service providers can de-escalate tensions and build consensus with clients. Transparent communication also helps to rebuild trust and repair damaged relationships, ensuring that both parties can move forward with confidence and clarity.

In conclusion, clear and transparent communication is indispensable for navigating unrealistic budget expectations and fostering successful client relationships. By establishing trust, managing expectations, aligning objectives, building rapport, and resolving conflicts, service providers can effectively navigate budgetary constraints while delivering value and achieving mutually satisfactory outcomes. Through proactive and transparent communication, service providers can build strong, lasting partnerships with their clients, laying the foundation for long-term success and mutual growth.

ii. Techniques For Articulating Budget Constraints Without Damaging Client Relationships.

Navigating budget constraints can be a delicate balance for service providers, particularly when communicating with clients who may have unrealistic expectations. Effectively articulating budget constraints is essential for managing client expectations, fostering trust, and maintaining positive relationships. In this section, we'll explore techniques for communicating budget constraints with clients in a way that is clear, transparent, and respectful, while minimizing the risk of damaging the client relationship.

1. Set Expectations Early:

One of the most effective techniques for articulating budget constraints is to set expectations early in the client engagement process. From the initial consultation or proposal stage, clearly communicate the parameters of the project, including budgetary constraints, scope of work, and anticipated timelines. By proactively addressing budget constraints upfront, you establish a foundation of transparency and trust, ensuring that both parties are aligned from the outset.

Setting expectations early also provides clients with an opportunity to ask questions, seek clarification, and adjust their expectations accordingly. This proactive approach demonstrates your commitment to open communication and helps to prevent misunderstandings or disagreements down the line.

2. Frame Budget Constraints Positively:

When communicating budget constraints with clients, it's important to frame the conversation in a positive light. Instead of focusing solely on what cannot be achieved within the budget, highlight the opportunities and benefits of working within the allocated budget. Emphasize the value proposition of your services and how they can help the client achieve their goals and objectives effectively and efficiently.

For example, instead of saying, "We can't do that within your budget," you could say, "Here's what we can accomplish within your budget, and here are the benefits of focusing on these priorities." By reframing the conversation in a positive and solution-oriented manner, you can help clients see the value in working within budget constraints and minimize the risk of damaging the client relationship.

3. Provide Context and Justification:

When communicating budget constraints with clients, provide context and justification for your proposed budget. Explain the factors that contribute to the cost of the project, such as the scope of work, level of complexity, and resources required. Break down the costs in a transparent manner, outlining how each component contributes to the overall budget.

Additionally, highlight the potential risks and consequences of deviating from the proposed budget, such as compromised quality, delays, or additional costs. By providing context and justification for your proposed budget, you help clients understand the rationale behind your recommendations and build trust in your expertise and professionalism.

4. Offer Alternatives and Solutions:

Instead of simply presenting budget constraints as a barrier to achieving the client's goals, offer alternatives and solutions that can help meet their needs within the allocated budget. This could involve prioritizing deliverables, phasing the project over time, or exploring creative solutions that deliver maximum value within budgetary constraints.

For example, if a client's budget cannot accommodate all the features they desire for a website redesign, you could propose a phased approach where essential features are implemented first, followed by additional features in subsequent phases as budget allows. By offering alternatives and solutions, you demonstrate flexibility and a commitment to finding mutually beneficial outcomes for both parties.

5. Maintain Open Lines of Communication:

Throughout the project lifecycle, maintain open lines of communication with the client to keep them informed and involved in decision-making processes. Provide regular updates on project progress, budgetary status, and any changes or challenges that may arise.

Encourage clients to ask questions, provide feedback, and raise concerns as they arise. By fostering a culture of open communication, you demonstrate your commitment to transparency and accountability, and minimize the risk of misunderstandings or conflicts related to budget constraints.

6. Focus on Value and Impact:

When communicating budget constraints with clients, focus on the value and impact of your services rather than just the cost. Highlight the potential benefits and outcomes that the client can expect to achieve by investing in your services, and how these align with their overall goals and objectives.

For example, instead of focusing solely on the cost of a marketing campaign, emphasize the potential return on investment (ROI) and the long-term value of building brand awareness, generating leads, and driving sales. By framing the conversation in terms of value and impact, you help clients see beyond the immediate costs and understand the broader benefits of working with you.

In conclusion, effectively articulating budget constraints is essential for managing client expectations, fostering trust, and maintaining positive relationships. By setting expectations early, framing budget constraints positively, providing context and justification, offering alternatives and solutions, maintaining open lines of communication, and focusing on value and impact, service providers can communicate budget constraints with clients in a way that minimizes the risk of damaging the client relationship while ensuring alignment and mutual understanding. Through proactive and transparent communication, service providers can navigate budget constraints successfully and deliver value to their clients effectively and efficiently.

^^^^

iii. Establishing Open Channels For Dialogue And Feedback.

In the realm of client relationships, establishing open channels for dialogue and feedback is crucial for fostering transparency, trust, and collaboration. Effective communication is a two-way street, and creating an environment where clients feel comfortable expressing their thoughts, concerns, and feedback is essential for building strong, lasting relationships. In this section, we'll explore the importance of establishing open channels for dialogue and feedback with clients and provide strategies for facilitating constructive communication.

1. Promoting Transparency:

Open channels for dialogue and feedback are instrumental in promoting transparency between service providers and clients. By creating opportunities for open and honest communication, you demonstrate your commitment to transparency and accountability, laying the foundation for trust and mutual understanding.

Transparency encompasses sharing relevant information about project progress, budgetary status, and any challenges or changes that may arise. By keeping clients informed and involved in decision-making processes, you empower them to make informed choices and feel confident in the partnership.

2. Building Trust:

Effective communication is fundamental to building trust with clients. When clients feel heard, valued, and respected, they are more likely to trust the expertise and integrity of the service provider. Establishing open channels for dialogue and feedback allows clients to express their thoughts, concerns, and feedback openly, fostering a sense of trust and partnership.

Building trust also involves being responsive and proactive in addressing client needs and concerns. By demonstrating your commitment to client satisfaction and success, you strengthen the client-provider relationship and lay the groundwork for long-term collaboration and mutual growth.

3. Encouraging Collaboration:

Open channels for dialogue and feedback facilitate collaboration between service providers and clients. By soliciting input and feedback from clients throughout the project lifecycle, you create opportunities for collaboration and co-creation, ensuring that the final deliverables meet the client's needs and expectations.

Encouraging collaboration also involves actively listening to clients' ideas, preferences, and goals, and incorporating their input into the project planning and execution process. By involving clients in decision-making processes and valuing their contributions, you foster a sense of ownership and investment in the project outcomes.

4. Providing Opportunities for Input:

Establishing open channels for dialogue and feedback requires providing clients with opportunities to share their thoughts, concerns, and feedback. This could involve conducting regular check-in meetings, setting up dedicated communication channels (such as email, phone calls, or project management platforms), or creating feedback surveys or forms.

When providing opportunities for input, it's essential to make the process as accessible and user-friendly as possible. Clearly communicate how clients can provide feedback, and ensure that they feel comfortable expressing their thoughts and opinions openly and honestly.

5. Actively Listening:

Effective communication involves not only sharing information but also actively listening to clients' concerns and feedback. Actively listening requires giving clients your full attention, being empathetic and nonjudgmental, and seeking to understand their perspective fully.

When clients share their thoughts or concerns, acknowledge their feelings and experiences, and validate their perspective. Reflect back what you've heard to ensure clarity and understanding, and ask clarifying questions to gain deeper insights into their needs and preferences.

6. Responding Thoughtfully:

In addition to actively listening, responding thoughtfully to client feedback is essential for building trust and fostering constructive communication. When clients share their concerns or suggestions, respond promptly and thoughtfully, acknowledging their input and addressing any issues or questions they may have.

When responding to client feedback, strive to be transparent, honest, and respectful. If changes or adjustments are needed, clearly communicate the rationale behind the decision and how it aligns with the client's goals and objectives. By responding thoughtfully to client feedback, you demonstrate your commitment to client satisfaction and success, and reinforce trust and confidence in the partnership.

In conclusion, establishing open channels for dialogue and feedback is essential for fostering transparency, trust, and collaboration with clients. By promoting transparency, building trust, encouraging collaboration, providing opportunities for input, actively listening, and responding thoughtfully, service providers can create an environment where clients feel valued, heard, and respected. Through proactive and constructive communication, service providers can strengthen client relationships, ensure alignment and understanding, and ultimately, deliver value and achieve mutual success.

3. Setting Realistic Expectations

Welcome to Chapter 3 of our book, where we explore the critical importance of setting realistic expectations when dealing with clients and their budget constraints. In this chapter, we delve into the strategies and techniques for effectively managing client expectations, aligning project scope with budgetary constraints, and fostering a collaborative and transparent approach to project management.

Setting realistic expectations is essential for ensuring the success and satisfaction of both parties involved in a client-service provider relationship. By establishing clear boundaries, defining achievable goals, and managing client perceptions, service providers can navigate budget constraints more effectively while delivering value and maintaining positive relationships with clients.

Join us as we explore the intricacies of setting realistic expectations, providing practical insights and actionable tips for service providers to navigate budget constraints with confidence, transparency, and professionalism. Through proactive communication and strategic planning, service providers can set the stage for successful collaborations that meet clients' needs while respecting budgetary limitations.

^^^^

i. Educating Clients About Industry Standards And Typical Costs.

In the dynamic landscape of business interactions, educating clients about industry standards and typical costs is a crucial component of managing expectations, fostering transparency, and building trust. In this section, we'll delve into the importance of educating clients about industry standards and typical costs, explore the benefits of doing so, and provide strategies for effectively communicating this information to clients.

1. Importance of Education:

Educating clients about industry standards and typical costs is essential for ensuring that they have realistic expectations regarding the scope, complexity, and cost of projects. Many clients may not be familiar with the intricacies of a particular industry or the typical costs associated with specific services or deliverables. By providing education and insight into industry norms and best practices, service providers empower clients to make informed decisions and set realistic budgets and expectations.

Furthermore, educating clients about industry standards helps to level the playing field and foster a more equitable and transparent client-service provider relationship. When clients have a better understanding of the factors that contribute to project costs and timelines, they are less likely to harbor unrealistic expectations or make unreasonable demands. Instead, they can collaborate more effectively with service providers to develop realistic project plans that align with their goals and constraints.

2. Benefits of Education:

There are several benefits to educating clients about industry standards and typical costs:

<u>Alignment of Expectations:</u> Educating clients about industry standards helps to align their expectations with reality. By providing insight into what is achievable within a given budget and timeframe, service providers can ensure that clients have realistic expectations regarding project scope, deliverables, and outcomes.

<u>Transparency and Trust:</u> Educating clients about industry standards fosters transparency and trust in the client-service provider relationship. When clients feel informed and knowledgeable about the factors that influence project costs and timelines, they are more likely to trust the expertise and recommendations of the service provider. This transparency builds confidence and credibility, laying the foundation for a positive and collaborative partnership.

<u>Mitigation of Disputes:</u> Educating clients about industry standards can help to mitigate disputes and conflicts that may arise during the project lifecycle. When clients have a clear understanding of the factors that contribute to project costs and timelines, they are less likely to dispute invoices or challenge proposed budgets. Instead, they can collaborate with service providers to address any concerns or discrepancies proactively, minimizing the risk of misunderstandings or disagreements.

3. Strategies for Communication:

Effectively communicating industry standards and typical costs to clients requires a strategic and thoughtful approach. Here are some strategies for communicating this information effectively:

<u>Use Plain Language:</u> Avoid technical jargon and industry-specific terminology when communicating with clients. Instead, use plain language and simple explanations to convey complex concepts and ideas. This ensures that clients understand the information being presented and feel comfortable asking questions or seeking clarification.

<u>Provide Examples and Case Studies:</u> Use real-world examples and case studies to illustrate industry standards and typical costs. Showcasing past projects or similar engagements can help clients visualize the scope, complexity, and cost of their own project, making the information more tangible and relatable.

Offer Comparative Analysis: Provide comparative analysis of industry benchmarks and best practices to give clients context for understanding project costs and timelines. This could include benchmarking data, industry reports, or comparative analysis of similar projects within the client's industry or market segment.

Be Transparent About Limitations: Be transparent about the limitations of industry standards and typical costs. While these benchmarks provide valuable insight, they are not prescriptive and may vary depending on the unique circumstances of each project. Clearly communicate any caveats or limitations associated with industry standards to ensure that clients have realistic expectations.

Encourage Questions and Dialogue: Encourage clients to ask questions and engage in dialogue about industry standards and typical costs. Create an open and welcoming environment where clients feel comfortable seeking clarification or expressing concerns. By fostering open communication and dialogue, service providers can address any misconceptions or misunderstandings that may arise and ensure that clients feel informed and empowered to make decisions.

In conclusion, educating clients about industry standards and typical costs is essential for managing expectations, fostering transparency, and building trust in the client-service provider relationship. By providing education and insight into industry norms and best practices, service providers empower clients to make informed decisions, set realistic budgets and expectations, and collaborate more effectively on projects. Through strategic communication and a commitment to transparency, service providers can ensure that clients have a clear understanding of the factors that influence project costs and timelines, laying the foundation for successful collaborations and mutual success.

∧∧∧∧

ii. Managing Client Perceptions And Assumptions About Project Scope.

In the realm of client relationships, managing perceptions and assumptions about project scope is essential for ensuring alignment, minimizing misunderstandings, and fostering successful collaborations. In this section, we'll delve into the importance of managing client perceptions and assumptions, explore common challenges that arise in this area, and provide strategies for effectively navigating these challenges to achieve mutual understanding and satisfaction.

1. Importance of Managing Perceptions:

Managing client perceptions about project scope is critical for setting expectations, mitigating misunderstandings, and avoiding scope creep. Clients may come into a project with preconceived notions or assumptions about what can be achieved within a given budget or timeframe. These perceptions can lead to unrealistic expectations, dissatisfaction, and conflicts if not addressed proactively.

By managing client perceptions effectively, service providers can ensure that clients have a clear understanding of the project scope, deliverables, and limitations. This sets the stage for productive collaboration and helps to prevent scope creep, budget overruns, and other issues that can derail a project.

2. Common Challenges:

Several common challenges arise when it comes to managing client perceptions and assumptions about project scope:

Unclear Communication: Poor communication can lead to misunderstandings and misinterpretations of project scope. Clients may assume that certain features or deliverables are included in the project scope when they are not explicitly outlined, leading to disagreements and conflicts later on.

Scope Creep: Scope creep occurs when additional features or requirements are added to the project scope without proper evaluation of their impact on budget, timeline, and resources. Clients may request changes or additions to the project scope midstream, assuming that they can be accommodated within the original parameters of the project.

Budget Constraints: Clients may have unrealistic assumptions about what can be achieved within their budget constraints. They may expect extensive features or deliverables that are not feasible within the allocated budget, leading to dissatisfaction when their expectations are not met.

3. Strategies for Effective Management:

Effectively managing client perceptions and assumptions about project scope requires a proactive and strategic approach. Here are some strategies for navigating this challenge:

Clarify Expectations Early: From the outset of the project, clearly communicate the scope, deliverables, and limitations to the client. Set expectations early and ensure that both parties have a shared understanding of what will be included in the project scope and what will not.

Document Scope Changes: If changes or additions to the project scope arise during the course of the project, document them carefully and assess their impact on budget, timeline, and resources. Communicate any scope changes to the client promptly and discuss the implications for the project.

Educate Clients About Trade-offs: Help clients understand the trade-offs involved in project scope decisions, such as the impact on budget, timeline, and resources. Educate them about the consequences of adding additional features or requirements to the project scope and encourage them to prioritize their needs accordingly.

Provide Regular Updates: Maintain open lines of communication with the client throughout the project lifecycle and provide regular updates on project progress, milestones, and any changes to the project scope. By keeping the client informed and involved in decision-making processes, you can ensure that they are aware of any deviations from the original scope and can provide input or feedback as needed.

Manage Expectations Proactively: Anticipate potential misunderstandings or assumptions about project scope and address them proactively. If you sense that the client has unrealistic expectations or assumptions about what can be achieved within the project scope, have a candid conversation with them to clarify any misconceptions and align expectations.

4. Foster Collaboration and Flexibility:

Finally, foster a spirit of collaboration and flexibility when managing client perceptions and assumptions about project scope. Encourage open dialogue and feedback, and be willing to listen to the client's concerns or suggestions. Be flexible and responsive to changes in the project scope, but also be firm in communicating the limitations and constraints that may affect the feasibility of certain requests.

In conclusion, managing client perceptions and assumptions about project scope is essential for ensuring successful collaborations and achieving mutual understanding and satisfaction. By clarifying expectations early, documenting scope changes, educating clients about trade-offs, providing regular updates, and fostering collaboration and flexibility, service providers can navigate this challenge effectively and ensure that both parties have a clear understanding of the project scope and objectives. Through proactive communication and strategic management, service providers can build strong, lasting relationships with their clients and deliver projects that meet their needs and expectations.

∧∧∧∧

iii. Strategies For Aligning Client Expectations With Budget Limitations.

Aligning client expectations with budget limitations is a delicate balancing act that requires strategic communication, proactive planning, and a collaborative approach. In this section, we'll explore effective strategies for navigating this challenge, ensuring that clients have realistic expectations regarding project scope, deliverables, and costs while maintaining transparency, trust, and satisfaction.

1. Establish Clear Communication Channels:

The foundation of aligning client expectations with budget limitations lies in establishing clear communication channels from the outset. Ensure that clients understand the parameters of the project, including the allocated budget, timeline, and scope of work. Provide opportunities for open dialogue and feedback, allowing clients to ask questions, express concerns, and share their goals and priorities.

By fostering open communication channels, service providers can proactively address any misconceptions or unrealistic expectations that clients may have regarding project scope and costs. This sets the stage for a collaborative and transparent client-service provider relationship, where both parties work together to achieve mutually beneficial outcomes.

2. Educate Clients About Industry Standards and Best Practices:

Many clients may not be familiar with industry standards and best practices regarding project scope and costs. Educating clients about these standards can help to manage their expectations and ensure that they have a realistic understanding of what can be achieved within their budget limitations.

Provide clients with insight into typical costs associated with similar projects, industry benchmarks, and factors that influence project scope and costs. Help them understand the trade-offs involved in project decisions, such as the impact on quality, timeline, and resources. By educating clients about industry standards and best practices, service providers empower them to make informed decisions and set realistic expectations.

3. Prioritize Deliverables and Features:

When working within budget limitations, it's essential to prioritize deliverables and features based on their importance and impact on project goals. Collaborate with clients to identify their top priorities and key objectives for the project, and focus resources and efforts on delivering those outcomes.

Encourage clients to prioritize deliverables based on their value and impact on the project's success. Help them understand that focusing on essential features and functionalities can maximize the return on investment and ensure that the project stays within budget constraints. By prioritizing deliverables and features, service providers can align client expectations with budget limitations while still delivering value and achieving project goals.

4. Offer Creative Solutions and Alternatives:

When faced with budget limitations, service providers can offer creative solutions and alternatives to help clients achieve their goals within their budget constraints. Explore different approaches, technologies, or methodologies that can deliver value while keeping costs in check.

Encourage clients to think creatively about how to achieve their objectives within budget limitations. For example, they may be able to leverage existing resources or assets, streamline processes, or focus on high-impact initiatives that yield maximum results with minimal investment. By offering creative solutions and alternatives, service providers demonstrate flexibility and a commitment to finding mutually beneficial outcomes.

5. Provide Transparent Cost Estimates and Breakdowns:

Transparency is key when aligning client expectations with budget limitations. Provide clients with transparent cost estimates and breakdowns that clearly outline the expenses associated with the project, including labor, materials, and any additional costs or fees.

Help clients understand the factors that contribute to project costs and how their budget will be allocated across different aspects of the project. Be upfront about any potential risks or uncertainties that may affect project costs and timelines, and discuss strategies for mitigating these risks.

By providing transparent cost estimates and breakdowns, service providers empower clients to make informed decisions about their project investments and ensure that their expectations align with budget limitations.

6. Manage Scope Changes Effectively:

Scope changes are inevitable in any project, but they can pose challenges when working within budget limitations. Effectively managing scope changes involves assessing their impact on budget, timeline, and resources, and communicating any adjustments to the client promptly.

When faced with scope changes, engage in open dialogue with the client to discuss the implications and explore potential solutions. Help them understand the trade-offs involved in accommodating scope changes within the existing budget and timeline constraints. By managing scope changes effectively, service providers can ensure that client expectations remain aligned with budget limitations throughout the project lifecycle.

In conclusion, aligning client expectations with budget limitations requires proactive communication, strategic planning, and a collaborative approach. By establishing clear communication channels, educating clients about industry standards and best practices, prioritizing deliverables and features, offering creative solutions and alternatives, providing transparent cost estimates and breakdowns, and managing scope changes effectively, service providers can ensure that clients have realistic expectations regarding project scope, deliverables, and costs. Through transparent and collaborative communication, service providers can build trust, foster satisfaction, and achieve successful outcomes for both parties involved.

4. Negotiating With Confidence.

Welcome to Chapter 4 of our book, where we delve into the intricacies of navigating negotiations and compromises with clients when dealing with budget limitations. In this chapter, we'll explore the art of negotiation, effective strategies for finding compromises, and maintaining positive client relationships while staying true to your business objectives.

Negotiating with clients over budget constraints can be a challenging yet necessary aspect of running a successful business. It requires finesse, empathy, and clear communication to find solutions that meet both the client's needs and the service provider's bottom line. Through proactive negotiation techniques and a commitment to finding mutually beneficial outcomes, service providers can navigate budget limitations with confidence and professionalism.

Join us as we explore practical tips, real-world examples, and actionable insights for navigating negotiations and compromises with clients, ensuring that projects stay on track, budgets remain manageable, and relationships thrive. Through effective negotiation strategies and a collaborative approach, service providers can turn budget constraints into opportunities for innovation, creativity, and growth.

∧∧∧∧

i. Identifying Areas For Negotiation And Compromise.

Navigating budget constraints often involves identifying areas where negotiation and compromise can occur. By strategically assessing project requirements, priorities, and client expectations, service providers can pinpoint opportunities for finding mutually beneficial solutions that balance budget limitations with project goals. In this section, we'll explore effective strategies for identifying areas for negotiation and compromise with clients.

1. Scope of Work:

The scope of work is often a prime area for negotiation and compromise when dealing with budget constraints. Service providers can work with clients to prioritize deliverables based on their importance and impact on project goals. By focusing on essential features and functionalities, both parties can ensure that project objectives are met while staying within budget limitations.

For example, if a client's budget cannot accommodate all the features they desire for a website redesign, the service provider can work with the client to identify the most critical features and functionalities and develop a phased approach for implementation. This allows the client to prioritize their needs while staying within budget constraints, and provides opportunities for future enhancements as budget allows.

2. Timeline:

Negotiating the project timeline is another area where compromise may be necessary when working within budget limitations. Clients may have tight deadlines or time-sensitive objectives that need to be accommodated, but these may conflict with the resources or time required to complete the project within budget.

Service providers can work with clients to develop realistic timelines that balance project requirements with budget constraints. This may involve adjusting milestones, reallocating resources, or streamlining processes to meet project deadlines while staying within budget limitations. By negotiating the project timeline, both parties can ensure that project objectives are achieved in a timely manner without compromising quality or budget.

3. Resources:

Resource allocation is a critical aspect of project planning and execution, particularly when working within budget limitations. Service providers may need to negotiate resource allocation with clients to ensure that the necessary personnel, equipment, and materials are available to complete the project successfully.

For example, if a client's budget cannot accommodate the full-time dedication of a project manager, the service provider may negotiate a part-time arrangement or explore alternative staffing solutions to meet the client's needs within budget constraints. By negotiating resource allocation, both parties can ensure that the project has the necessary resources to succeed while staying within budget limitations.

4. Deliverables:

Negotiating deliverables is another key area where compromise may be necessary when dealing with budget constraints. Clients may have specific expectations regarding project deliverables, but these may need to be adjusted or prioritized based on budget limitations.

Service providers can work with clients to identify the most critical deliverables and develop a phased approach for delivery based on budget constraints. This allows both parties to focus on achieving the most important outcomes first, while providing opportunities for additional deliverables in the future as budget allows. By negotiating deliverables, service providers can ensure that project objectives are met while staying within budget limitations.

5. Quality Assurance:

Maintaining quality standards is essential for project success, but this may require negotiation and compromise when working within budget limitations. Clients may have expectations regarding the level of quality or standards of workmanship, but these may need to be adjusted or aligned with budget constraints.

Service providers can negotiate quality assurance measures with clients to ensure that project objectives are met while staying within budget limitations. This may involve defining clear quality criteria, establishing checkpoints or milestones for quality assurance, and implementing feedback mechanisms to address any concerns or issues that arise. By negotiating quality assurance measures, both parties can ensure that project deliverables meet the necessary standards while staying within budget limitations.

6. Communication and Reporting:

Effective communication and reporting are essential for project success, but these may require negotiation and compromise when working within budget limitations. Clients may have expectations regarding the frequency and format of communication and reporting, but these may need to be adjusted or aligned with budget constraints.

Service providers can negotiate communication and reporting protocols with clients to ensure that project objectives are met while staying within budget limitations. This may involve defining clear communication channels, establishing regular reporting schedules, and aligning expectations regarding the level of detail and format of reports. By negotiating communication and reporting protocols, both parties can ensure that project progress is effectively monitored and communicated while staying within budget limitations.

In conclusion, identifying areas for negotiation and compromise is essential for navigating budget constraints and achieving project success. By strategically assessing project requirements, priorities, and client expectations, service providers can pinpoint opportunities for finding mutually beneficial solutions that balance budget limitations with project goals. Through effective negotiation and compromise, both parties can ensure that project objectives are met while maintaining transparency, trust, and satisfaction.

^^^^

ii. Presenting Alternative Solutions Within Budget Constraints.

In the dynamic landscape of client relationships, presenting alternative solutions within budget constraints is a strategic imperative for service providers. When faced with budget limitations, offering creative alternatives demonstrates flexibility, innovation, and a commitment to finding mutually beneficial outcomes. In this section, we'll explore effective strategies for presenting alternative solutions that meet client needs while staying within budget constraints.

1. Understand Client Needs and Goals:

Before presenting alternative solutions, it's crucial to have a thorough understanding of the client's needs, goals, and priorities. Take the time to engage in meaningful dialogue with the client to uncover their objectives, challenges, and constraints. Ask probing questions to gain insights into what they hope to achieve with the project and what factors are most important to them.

By understanding the client's needs and goals, service providers can tailor alternative solutions to address specific pain points and deliver maximum value within budget constraints. This client-centric approach demonstrates empathy and a commitment to meeting the client's objectives, laying the foundation for a collaborative and successful partnership.

2. Evaluate Cost-Effective Technologies and Methodologies:

One strategy for presenting alternative solutions within budget constraints is to explore cost-effective technologies and methodologies that can deliver value without breaking the bank. Research innovative tools, platforms, or approaches that offer efficient solutions to common challenges or streamline project workflows.

For example, leveraging open-source software, cloud-based solutions, or automation tools can help reduce development costs and improve efficiency without sacrificing quality. Similarly, adopting agile methodologies or lean practices can enable faster delivery of project outcomes while minimizing waste and unnecessary expenses.

By evaluating cost-effective technologies and methodologies, service providers can present alternative solutions that align with budget constraints while still meeting client objectives and expectations.

3. Prioritize Features and Functionality:

When working within budget constraints, it's essential to prioritize features and functionality based on their importance and impact on project goals. Collaborate with the client to identify their top priorities and key objectives for the project, and focus resources and efforts on delivering those outcomes.

Encourage clients to prioritize features and functionality based on their value and impact on the project's success. Help them understand that focusing on essential features can maximize the return on investment and ensure that the project stays within budget constraints.

By prioritizing features and functionality, service providers can present alternative solutions that deliver the most value to the client while staying within budget limitations.

4. Offer Phased Approaches and Iterative Solutions:

Another strategy for presenting alternative solutions within budget constraints is to offer phased approaches or iterative solutions that allow for incremental progress over time. Instead of trying to deliver everything at once, break the project down into smaller, manageable phases that can be completed within budget limitations.

For example, instead of building a complex system with all the bells and whistles upfront, start with a minimum viable product (MVP) that addresses core functionalities and can be deployed quickly and cost-effectively.

Subsequent phases can then focus on adding additional features and enhancements based on user feedback and evolving requirements.

By offering phased approaches and iterative solutions, service providers can present alternative solutions that deliver tangible results while staying within budget constraints and mitigating risk.

5. Explore Outsourcing and Collaborative Partnerships:

In some cases, presenting alternative solutions within budget constraints may involve outsourcing certain tasks or collaborating with third-party vendors or partners. Explore opportunities to leverage external expertise, resources, or capabilities that can complement your own and enhance project outcomes.

For example, outsourcing non-core activities such as graphic design, content creation, or quality assurance testing to specialized vendors can help reduce costs and improve efficiency. Similarly, forming strategic partnerships with other service providers or technology partners can enable access to additional resources or capabilities that may not be available in-house.

By exploring outsourcing and collaborative partnerships, service providers can present alternative solutions that leverage external expertise and resources while staying within budget constraints.

6. Communicate Value Proposition and Benefits:

When presenting alternative solutions within budget constraints, it's essential to communicate the value proposition and benefits effectively to the client. Clearly articulate how the proposed solution addresses their needs, solves their challenges, and delivers tangible benefits that align with their objectives.

Highlight the cost savings, efficiency gains, or competitive advantages that the alternative solution offers compared to other options. Provide real-world examples, case studies, or testimonials that demonstrate the effectiveness of the proposed approach and its potential impact on the client's business.

By communicating the value proposition and benefits, service providers can build confidence and trust with the client and increase their willingness to consider alternative solutions within budget constraints.

In conclusion, presenting alternative solutions within budget constraints requires creativity, innovation, and strategic thinking. By understanding client needs and goals, evaluating cost-effective technologies and methodologies, prioritizing features and functionality, offering phased approaches and iterative solutions, exploring outsourcing and collaborative partnerships, and communicating the value proposition and benefits effectively, service providers can present alternative solutions that meet client needs while staying within budget limitations. Through proactive and collaborative engagement, service providers can navigate budget constraints successfully and deliver value to their clients effectively and efficiently.

∧∧∧∧

iii. Tips For Maintaining Professionalism And Assertiveness During Negotiations.

Negotiations are a fundamental aspect of client interactions, particularly when navigating budget constraints and project scope. Maintaining professionalism and assertiveness during negotiations is crucial for ensuring that both parties achieve mutually beneficial outcomes while preserving the integrity of the client-service provider relationship. In this section, we'll explore effective tips for staying professional and assertive during negotiations.

1. Prepare Thoroughly:

Preparation is key to maintaining professionalism and assertiveness during negotiations. Take the time to research and gather relevant information about the client, their industry, and their specific needs and goals. Anticipate potential objections or concerns that may arise during negotiations and develop strategies for addressing them effectively.

Prepare a clear agenda and objectives for the negotiation meeting, outlining the key points to be discussed and the desired outcomes. By being well-prepared, you'll feel more confident and empowered to assertively advocate for your position while maintaining professionalism and composure.

2. Listen Actively:

Effective negotiation requires active listening and empathy. Take the time to listen to the client's concerns, needs, and priorities without interrupting or jumping to conclusions. Demonstrate empathy and understanding by acknowledging their perspective and validating their feelings and experiences.

Active listening not only helps to build rapport and trust with the client but also provides valuable insights into their motivations and priorities. By understanding the client's underlying needs and concerns, you can tailor your negotiation strategy to address them effectively and achieve mutually beneficial outcomes.

3. Communicate Clearly and Concisely:

Clear and concise communication is essential for maintaining professionalism and assertiveness during negotiations. Clearly articulate your position, interests, and objectives using language that is straightforward and easy to understand. Avoid ambiguity or confusion by providing specific examples, data, or evidence to support your arguments.

Be assertive but respectful in your communication style, expressing your views and concerns confidently while acknowledging the perspectives of others. Use "I" statements to take ownership of your thoughts and feelings, and avoid blaming or criticizing the other party.

4. Set Boundaries and Limits:

Maintaining professionalism and assertiveness during negotiations requires setting clear boundaries and limits. Know your priorities and non-negotiables going into the negotiation, and be prepared to assertively defend them if necessary. Communicate your boundaries and limits to the client in a firm but respectful manner, and be prepared to walk away from the negotiation if they are not respected.

Setting boundaries and limits helps to establish your credibility and integrity as a negotiator, signaling to the client that you are serious about achieving mutually beneficial outcomes while preserving your own interests and priorities.

5. Focus on Win-Win Solutions:

Negotiations are not about winning or losing but about finding mutually beneficial solutions that satisfy the interests and objectives of both parties. Maintain a collaborative mindset throughout the negotiation process, focusing on creating win-win outcomes that address the needs and concerns of both parties.

Look for creative solutions and compromises that allow both parties to achieve their goals while staying within budget constraints and preserving the integrity of the project. Be open to exploring alternative options and flexible in your approach, and encourage the client to do the same.

6. Stay Calm and Professional:

Finally, maintaining professionalism and assertiveness during negotiations requires staying calm, composed, and professional, even in the face of challenges or disagreements. Avoid getting emotional or defensive, and instead, respond to conflict or resistance with poise and professionalism.

Take breaks if necessary to collect your thoughts and regain perspective, and avoid making impulsive decisions or concessions that may compromise your interests. Focus on finding common ground and building rapport with the client, even if there are differences of opinion or conflicting priorities.

In conclusion, maintaining professionalism and assertiveness during negotiations is essential for achieving mutually beneficial outcomes while preserving the integrity of the client-service provider relationship. By preparing thoroughly, listening actively, communicating clearly and concisely, setting boundaries and limits, focusing on win-win solutions, and staying calm and professional, service providers can navigate negotiations effectively and achieve successful outcomes that meet the needs and objectives of both parties involved. Through proactive and assertive engagement, service providers can build trust, foster satisfaction, and lay the foundation for long-term collaboration and success.

5. Managing Scope Creep.

Welcome to Chapter 5 of our book, where we tackle the critical topic of managing scope creep in client projects. Scope creep, the gradual expansion of project scope beyond its original boundaries, is a common challenge faced by service providers. In this chapter, we'll explore the causes of scope creep, its impact on project outcomes, and effective strategies for prevention and management.

Scope creep can derail projects, lead to budget overruns, and strain client relationships if not addressed proactively. However, by understanding its root causes and implementing robust management strategies, service providers can mitigate its effects and ensure successful project delivery.

Join us as we delve into practical tips, real-world examples, and actionable insights for managing scope creep effectively. Through clear communication, proactive planning, and diligent scope management, service providers can navigate scope creep with confidence and deliver projects that meet client expectations while staying within budget and timeline constraints.

∧∧∧∧

I. Recognizing Signs Of Scope Creep And Its Impact On Budget And Timelines.

Recognizing Signs of Scope Creep and Its Impact on Budget and Timelines Scope creep, the gradual expansion of project scope beyond its original boundaries, is a pervasive challenge faced by service providers in client projects. Recognizing the signs of scope creep and understanding its impact on budget and timelines are crucial for effective project management and successful outcomes. In this section, we'll explore the common signs of scope creep and examine its detrimental effects on project budgets and timelines.

1. Signs of Scope Creep:

Recognizing the signs of scope creep is essential for identifying and addressing this phenomenon before it spirals out of control. Some common signs of scope creep include:

Unplanned Changes: When clients continuously request changes or additions to the project scope that were not included in the original agreement, it may indicate scope creep. These changes often result from evolving requirements, shifting priorities, or a lack of clarity in the project scope.

Feature Creep: Feature creep occurs when additional features or functionalities are added to the project scope without proper evaluation of their impact on budget and timelines. Clients may request additional bells and whistles that were not part of the initial project scope, leading to scope expansion and increased complexity.

Extended Deadlines: If project deadlines are repeatedly extended to accommodate new requirements or changes, it may be a sign of scope creep. Delays in project milestones or deliverables can indicate that the project scope has expanded beyond its original boundaries, requiring additional time and resources to complete.

Budget Overruns: Scope creep often leads to budget overruns as additional work or changes incur additional costs that were not accounted for in the original budget. If project expenditures exceed the initial budget estimates due to scope changes or unplanned work, it is a clear indication of scope creep.

2. Impact on Budget:

Scope creep can have a significant impact on project budgets, leading to cost overruns and financial strain for both service providers and clients. Some ways in which scope creep affects project budgets include:

Additional Work: Scope creep often results in the need for additional work or changes to accommodate new requirements or features. This additional work incurs additional costs in terms of labor, materials, and resources, which can quickly deplete the project budget.

Resource Allocation: As the project scope expands, resources may need to be reallocated or additional resources brought in to handle the increased workload. This can lead to higher labor costs, subcontractor fees, or overhead expenses that were not accounted for in the original budget.

Revisions and Rework: Scope creep may necessitate revisions or rework of existing work to accommodate new requirements or changes. This rework consumes additional time and resources, leading to increased costs and delays in project delivery.

Client Expectations: Budget overruns due to scope creep can strain client relationships and erode trust if clients feel that they are being charged for work that was not agreed upon or that the project is not being managed effectively. This can lead to dissatisfaction and reluctance to engage in future projects with the service provider.

3. Impact on Timelines:

Scope creep can also have a detrimental impact on project timelines, leading to delays and missed deadlines. Some ways in which scope creep affects project timelines include:

Extended Project Duration: Scope creep often results in an extended project duration as additional work or changes require more time to complete. Delays in project milestones or deliverables can push back the overall project timeline, leading to frustration and dissatisfaction among stakeholders.

Resource Constraints: As the project scope expands, resources may become stretched thin, leading to bottlenecks and delays in project execution. Limited availability of key personnel, equipment, or materials can impede progress and prolong the project timeline.

Revisions and Rework: Scope creep may necessitate revisions or rework of existing work, which can disrupt project flow and cause delays. Repeated revisions or rework cycles consume valuable time and resources, leading to schedule slippage and missed deadlines.

Client Expectations: Missed deadlines due to scope creep can damage client relationships and erode trust if clients feel that their project is not being managed effectively. Clients may become frustrated and disillusioned if promised milestones are not met, leading to dissatisfaction and potential disputes.

In conclusion, recognizing the signs of scope creep and understanding its impact on budget and timelines are crucial for effective project management and successful outcomes. By identifying early warning signs of scope creep and implementing robust scope management strategies, service providers can mitigate its effects and ensure that projects are delivered on time and within budget. Through proactive communication, diligent planning, and a commitment to managing scope effectively, service providers can navigate scope creep with confidence and deliver projects that meet client expectations and objectives.

∧∧∧∧

ii. Implementing Strategies To Prevent And Address Scope Creep Effectively.

Scope creep, the gradual expansion of project scope beyond its original boundaries, poses significant challenges for service providers in client projects. Preventing and addressing scope creep effectively requires proactive strategies and diligent scope management throughout the project lifecycle. In this section, we'll explore actionable strategies for both preventing and addressing scope creep to ensure successful project outcomes.

1. Establish Clear Project Scope:

One of the most effective strategies for preventing scope creep is to establish a clear and well-defined project scope from the outset. Work closely with the client to document project requirements, objectives, deliverables, and timelines in a comprehensive project scope statement. Ensure that all stakeholders have a shared understanding of the project scope and that expectations are aligned from the start.

By establishing clear project scope boundaries, service providers can minimize ambiguity and prevent misunderstandings that can lead to scope creep later on. Regularly review and update the project scope as needed throughout the project lifecycle to ensure that it remains relevant and aligned with client expectations.

2. Define Change Management Processes:

Implementing robust change management processes is essential for effectively managing scope changes and preventing scope creep. Establish clear procedures for evaluating, approving, and implementing changes to the project scope, including documentation requirements, approval authorities, and impact assessments.

Encourage clients to submit change requests through formal channels and provide them with a clear understanding of the process for evaluating and implementing changes. Ensure that all changes are assessed for their impact on budget, timelines, and resources before being approved, and communicate any implications to stakeholders promptly.

3. Set Realistic Deadlines and Milestones:

Setting realistic deadlines and milestones is crucial for preventing scope creep and maintaining project momentum. Work closely with the client to establish achievable project timelines based on the scope of work, resource availability, and project constraints. Break the project down into smaller milestones and deliverables to track progress and ensure accountability.

Avoid overcommitting to unrealistic deadlines or promising delivery dates without proper evaluation of project requirements and constraints. Be transparent with the client about the potential consequences of missed deadlines or delays and work collaboratively to adjust timelines as needed to accommodate changes or unforeseen challenges.

4. Monitor Project Progress Closely:

Regularly monitoring project progress is essential for identifying potential scope creep early and taking corrective action before it escalates. Implement robust project tracking and reporting mechanisms to monitor progress against project milestones, budgets, and deliverables.

Review project status reports, budget tracking sheets, and task lists regularly to identify any deviations from the project plan or signs of scope creep. If changes to the project scope are identified, assess their impact on budget, timelines, and resources, and take proactive steps to address them through formal change management processes.

5. Communicate Proactively with Stakeholders:

Effective communication with stakeholders is key to preventing and addressing scope creep effectively. Keep stakeholders informed about project progress, changes to the project scope, and any potential risks or challenges that may arise.

Encourage open dialogue and feedback from stakeholders throughout the project lifecycle, and address any concerns or questions promptly. Be transparent about the implications of scope changes on budget and timelines, and work collaboratively with stakeholders to find mutually acceptable solutions.

6. Be Prepared to Negotiate:

Despite proactive prevention efforts, scope creep may still occur in some projects. In such cases, be prepared to negotiate with the client to address scope changes while minimizing their impact on project outcomes.

Present alternative solutions or compromises that allow the client to achieve their objectives within budget and timeline constraints. Focus on finding win-win solutions that satisfy both parties' needs and preserve the integrity of the project.

7. Document Everything:

Finally, document all project-related communications, decisions, and changes to ensure accountability and transparency throughout the project lifecycle. Maintain a comprehensive project file that includes meeting minutes, change requests, correspondence, and any other relevant documentation.

Having a well-documented record of project activities and decisions can help mitigate disputes, resolve conflicts, and provide clarity in case of scope-related issues or challenges.

In conclusion, implementing strategies to prevent and address scope creep effectively requires proactive planning, clear communication, and diligent scope management throughout the project lifecycle. By establishing clear project scope, defining change management processes, setting realistic deadlines, monitoring project progress closely, communicating proactively with stakeholders, being prepared to negotiate, and documenting everything, service providers can minimize the risk of scope creep and ensure successful project outcomes. Through proactive and strategic scope management, service providers can deliver projects that meet client expectations and objectives while staying within budget and timeline constraints.

^^^^

iii. Communicating Changes In Scope To Clients And Managing Expectations.

Effective communication is paramount when it comes to navigating changes in project scope with clients. Whether it's accommodating new requirements or addressing unexpected challenges, transparent and proactive communication can mitigate misunderstandings and maintain trust. In this section, we'll explore strategies for effectively communicating changes in scope to clients and managing their expectations.

1. Transparency is Key:

Transparency should underpin all communication regarding changes in project scope. Be upfront with clients about any proposed changes, explaining the reasons behind them and the potential impact on the project. By providing clear and honest information, you build trust and foster a collaborative relationship with the client.

2. Timely Communication:

Timeliness is crucial when communicating changes in scope. As soon as you become aware of a potential change, inform the client promptly. Delayed communication can exacerbate the situation and lead to frustration on the client's part. Keeping the client informed at every stage demonstrates your commitment to transparency and accountability.

3. Explain the Rationale:

When presenting changes in scope to clients, it's essential to explain the rationale behind the proposed adjustments. Help the client understand why the change is necessary and how it aligns with project objectives. Providing context allows the client to see the bigger picture and makes them more receptive to the proposed changes.

4. Highlight Impact on Project:

Clearly articulate the impact of the proposed changes on the project, including any adjustments to timelines, budgets, and deliverables. Help the client understand the trade-offs involved in accommodating the new requirements or addressing the challenges. By being transparent about the consequences, you enable the client to make informed decisions.

5. Offer Solutions:

Instead of presenting changes in scope as problems, frame them as opportunities to enhance the project. Offer solutions or alternatives that mitigate the impact of the changes on the project's timeline and budget. Collaborate with the client to find the best course of action that balances their needs with project constraints.

6. Document Changes:

It's essential to document all changes in scope and obtain the client's approval in writing. This helps ensure clarity and avoid misunderstandings down the line. Create change orders or amendments to the project agreement that outline the revised scope, timelines, and budgets. Both parties should sign off on the changes to acknowledge their acceptance.

7. Manage Expectations:

Effective communication is also about managing expectations. Be realistic with the client about what can be achieved within the constraints of the project. If accommodating new requirements means extending timelines or increasing costs, communicate this clearly to the client. Managing expectations upfront minimizes the risk of disappointment later on.

8. Keep Lines of Communication Open:

Maintain open lines of communication with the client throughout the project. Encourage them to voice any concerns or questions they may have about the changes in scope. Actively listen to their feedback and address their concerns promptly. Regular communication builds trust and strengthens the client-service provider relationship.

9. Anticipate and Plan for Changes:

While it's impossible to predict every change that may arise during a project, proactive planning can help anticipate and mitigate potential risks. Conduct thorough risk assessments at the outset of the project to identify possible sources of scope creep. Develop contingency plans and allocate resources accordingly to address unforeseen changes as they arise.

10. Learn from Experience:

After each project, take the time to reflect on what worked well and what could be improved in terms of scope management and communication. Incorporate lessons learned into your processes and practices to enhance your ability to manage changes in scope effectively in future projects. Continuous improvement ensures that you're better equipped to navigate challenges and deliver successful outcomes for your clients.

In conclusion, effective communication is essential for navigating changes in project scope with clients. By being transparent, timely, and proactive in your communication, you can manage expectations and maintain trust throughout the project lifecycle. By offering solutions, managing expectations, and keeping lines of communication open, you can navigate changes in scope effectively and ensure successful project outcomes. Through continuous improvement and learning from experience, you can enhance your ability to manage changes in scope and deliver value to your clients consistently.

6. Building Long-Term Client Relationships.

Chapter 6 of our book focuses on the crucial aspect of building long-term client relationships. In this chapter, we'll explore the strategies, principles, and best practices for cultivating strong and enduring partnerships with clients. Long-term client relationships are the cornerstone of a successful business, offering stability, loyalty, and growth opportunities. Join us as we delve into the art of building lasting connections with clients, nurturing trust, and delivering value that goes beyond individual projects. Through proactive communication, exceptional service, and a commitment to client success, service providers can lay the foundation for mutually beneficial relationships that endure the test of time.

∧∧∧∧

i. Cultivating Trust And Credibility Through Transparency And Honesty.

Trust and credibility are the cornerstones of successful client relationships. In an increasingly competitive business landscape, clients seek partners they can rely on, ones who prioritize transparency and honesty in their interactions. Cultivating trust and credibility through transparency and honesty not only strengthens existing relationships but also fosters long-term partnerships built on mutual respect and integrity. In this section, we'll explore the importance of transparency and honesty in building trust and credibility with clients and examine practical strategies for incorporating these values into client interactions.

1. Establish Open Communication Channels:

Open communication is fundamental to building trust and credibility with clients. Establishing clear and accessible communication channels demonstrates your commitment to transparency and openness. Encourage clients to reach out with questions, concerns, or feedback at any time and respond promptly to their inquiries. By fostering an environment of open communication, you create opportunities for meaningful dialogue and collaboration, laying the foundation for a trusting relationship.

2. Be Honest About Limitations and Challenges:

Honesty is essential when discussing project limitations, challenges, or risks with clients. Instead of sugarcoating issues or downplaying challenges, be upfront and transparent about the realities of the situation. Acknowledge any potential obstacles or constraints that may impact project outcomes and work collaboratively with the client to develop strategies for addressing them. By demonstrating honesty and transparency, you build credibility and trust with clients, even in the face of adversity.

3. Set Realistic Expectations:

Managing client expectations is key to building trust and credibility. Be transparent about what can realistically be achieved within the scope of the project, considering factors such as timelines, budgets, and resource constraints. Avoid overpromising or making unrealistic commitments that may lead to disappointment later on. Instead, set clear and achievable expectations from the outset, ensuring alignment between client goals and project deliverables.

4. Share Insights and Expertise:

Sharing insights and expertise with clients demonstrates your commitment to adding value and helping them achieve their objectives. Be proactive in providing relevant information, industry insights, or best practices that may benefit the client. Share case studies, success stories, or examples of similar projects you've worked on to illustrate your capabilities and expertise. By sharing knowledge and insights openly, you position yourself as a trusted advisor and build credibility with clients.

5. Admit Mistakes and Take Ownership:

No one is perfect, and mistakes are inevitable in business. When mistakes occur, it's crucial to admit them openly and take ownership of the situation. Instead of making excuses or shifting blame, apologize sincerely and outline steps to rectify the issue. By demonstrating humility and accountability, you show clients that you value transparency and integrity, even when things don't go as planned. This level of honesty builds trust and strengthens the client-provider relationship.

6. Provide Regular Updates and Progress Reports:

Regular updates and progress reports are essential for maintaining transparency and keeping clients informed about project status and developments. Provide clients with regular updates on project milestones, achievements, and any challenges encountered along the way. Be proactive in communicating both positive news and potential setbacks, allowing clients to stay informed and involved in the project process. By providing transparent and timely updates, you build trust and confidence with clients, demonstrating your commitment to transparency and accountability.

7. Act with Integrity in all Interactions:

Above all, integrity should guide every interaction with clients. Act with honesty, fairness, and ethical conduct in all aspects of your business dealings. Honor commitments, uphold promises, and follow through on your obligations to clients. Avoid deceptive or unethical practices that compromise trust and credibility. By consistently acting with integrity, you establish a reputation for reliability and honesty that clients can trust and rely on for years to come.

In conclusion, cultivating trust and credibility through transparency and honesty is essential for building strong and lasting client relationships. By establishing open communication channels, being honest about limitations and challenges, setting realistic expectations, sharing insights and expertise, admitting mistakes and taking ownership, providing regular updates and progress reports, and acting with integrity in all interactions, service providers can build trust and credibility with clients, fostering long-term partnerships based on mutual respect and integrity. Through transparency and honesty, service providers can differentiate themselves in the marketplace, strengthen client loyalty, and position themselves for continued success in the long run.

∧∧∧∧

ii. Strategies For Exceeding Client Expectations While Staying Within Budget.

Exceeding client expectations while staying within budget is the hallmark of exceptional service delivery. It requires a delicate balance between delivering high-quality results and managing resources effectively. In this section, we'll explore practical strategies for surpassing client expectations while remaining mindful of budget constraints.

1. Understand Client Needs and Expectations:

The first step in exceeding client expectations is to have a thorough understanding of their needs, goals, and expectations. Take the time to engage with the client and gather insights into their vision for the project. Ask probing questions to uncover their preferences, priorities, and desired outcomes. By understanding the client's expectations upfront, you can tailor your approach to deliver results that resonate with their objectives.

2. Set Clear Expectations from the Outset:

Establishing clear expectations from the outset is crucial for managing client perceptions and ensuring alignment between deliverables and objectives. Clearly outline project scope, timelines, milestones, and deliverables in the initial project agreement. Communicate any limitations or constraints that may impact the project and discuss strategies for addressing them. By setting clear expectations upfront, you create a framework for success and minimize the risk of misunderstandings later on.

3. Focus on Value-Added Services:

Identify opportunities to provide value-added services that go above and beyond the client's expectations. Look for ways to add extra value to the project without significantly increasing costs. This could involve offering additional features, enhancements, or recommendations that enhance the overall value proposition for the client. By delivering unexpected value, you demonstrate your commitment to client success and differentiate yourself from competitors.

4. Emphasize Quality over Quantity:

Quality should always take precedence over quantity when it comes to exceeding client expectations. Focus on delivering high-quality results that meet or exceed the client's standards, even if it means scaling back on certain features or deliverables. Invest time and resources in thorough testing, quality assurance, and refinement to ensure that the final product meets the highest standards of excellence. By prioritizing quality, you enhance the perceived value of your services and build trust with the client.

5. Leverage Innovation and Creativity:

Innovation and creativity are powerful tools for exceeding client expectations while staying within budget. Look for innovative solutions, technologies, or methodologies that can deliver superior results more efficiently or cost-effectively. Brainstorm creative ideas and approaches that add unique value to the project and set you apart from competitors. By embracing innovation and creativity, you demonstrate your commitment to pushing the boundaries and delivering exceptional outcomes for the client.

6. Proactive Problem-Solving:

Anticipate potential challenges or obstacles that may arise during the project and develop proactive strategies for addressing them. Take a proactive approach to problem-solving, seeking solutions before issues escalate and impact project outcomes. Communicate openly with the client about any challenges encountered and collaborate on strategies for overcoming them. By demonstrating your ability to navigate obstacles effectively, you build confidence and trust with the client.

7. Foster a Culture of Continuous Improvement:

Continuous improvement is essential for exceeding client expectations over the long term. Encourage a culture of learning, innovation, and growth within your organization, where team members are empowered to identify opportunities for improvement and implement changes proactively. Solicit feedback from clients regularly and use it to inform process improvements and service enhancements. By continuously striving for excellence, you ensure that your services remain relevant, valuable, and aligned with client needs and expectations.

8. Communicate Value Effectively:

Finally, communicate the value of your services effectively to the client to ensure they recognize the benefits they're receiving. Highlight the unique value proposition of your offerings, emphasizing how they address the client's specific needs and deliver tangible benefits. Provide case studies, testimonials, or examples of past successes to illustrate the value you bring to the table. By communicating value effectively, you reinforce the client's confidence in your services and enhance their overall satisfaction.

In conclusion, exceeding client expectations while staying within budget requires a strategic approach that prioritizes understanding client needs, setting clear expectations, focusing on value-added services, emphasizing quality over quantity, leveraging innovation and creativity, proactive problem-solving, fostering a culture of continuous improvement, and communicating value effectively. By implementing these strategies, service providers can deliver exceptional results that exceed client expectations, build long-term relationships, and drive business success. Through proactive and client-focused engagement, service providers can differentiate themselves in the marketplace and position themselves as trusted partners for their clients' success.

∧∧∧∧

iii. Leveraging Positive Client Experiences For Repeat Business And Referrals.

Positive client experiences are invaluable assets that can drive repeat business and generate referrals, fostering long-term growth and success for service providers. By delivering exceptional service and exceeding client expectations, service providers can cultivate loyal clients who are eager to return for future projects and recommend their services to others. In this section, we'll explore effective strategies for leveraging positive client experiences to maximize repeat business and referrals.

1. Prioritize Client Satisfaction:

The foundation of positive client experiences lies in prioritizing client satisfaction at every stage of the engagement. Focus on understanding and addressing the unique needs and preferences of each client, ensuring that their expectations are not only met but exceeded. Regularly solicit feedback from clients to gauge satisfaction levels and identify areas for improvement. By prioritizing client satisfaction, you lay the groundwork for building strong and lasting relationships that drive repeat business and referrals.

2. Deliver Consistently High-Quality Service:

Consistency is key when it comes to delivering positive client experiences. Strive to consistently deliver high-quality service and results across all projects and interactions. Maintain rigorous standards of excellence in every aspect of your service delivery, from communication and responsiveness to the quality of workmanship. By consistently meeting or exceeding client expectations, you build trust and confidence, making clients more likely to return for future projects and recommend your services to others.

3. Exceed Expectations at Every Opportunity:

Going above and beyond to exceed client expectations is a powerful way to create memorable and positive experiences that drive repeat business and referrals. Look for opportunities to add extra value to the project, whether it's through innovative solutions, proactive problem-solving, or unexpected gestures of goodwill. Anticipate client needs and preferences, and strive to surpass their expectations in every interaction. By consistently exceeding expectations, you create loyal clients who are eager to work with you again and refer others to your services.

4. Build Strong Relationships Based on Trust and Respect:

Building strong relationships with clients based on trust and respect is essential for generating repeat business and referrals. Invest time and effort in getting to know your clients personally, understanding their goals, preferences, and challenges. Communicate openly and transparently, demonstrating integrity and reliability in all your interactions. By building strong relationships built on mutual trust and respect, you create a foundation of loyalty and advocacy that drives repeat business and referrals.

5. Stay Top of Mind with Regular Follow-Up:

Maintaining regular communication with clients is crucial for staying top of mind and encouraging repeat business and referrals. Follow up with clients after project completion to ensure their satisfaction and address any remaining concerns or questions. Stay in touch with clients through newsletters, updates, or relevant industry insights to keep them informed and engaged. By staying top of mind with regular follow-up, you remain a trusted and valued partner in their eyes, increasing the likelihood of repeat business and referrals.

6. Encourage and Incentivize Referrals:

Referrals are one of the most powerful sources of new business for service providers. Encourage and incentivize satisfied clients to refer their colleagues, friends, or contacts to your services. Offer referral incentives, such as discounts, rewards, or special offers, to clients who refer new business to you. Create a referral program that makes it easy for clients to refer others and rewards them for their advocacy. By leveraging the power of referrals, you tap into a valuable source of new business that stems from positive client experiences.

7. Showcase Success Stories and Testimonials:

Highlighting success stories and testimonials from satisfied clients is a compelling way to demonstrate the value of your services and attract new business. Showcase case studies, testimonials, or client success stories on your website, social media, or marketing materials to illustrate the positive outcomes clients have achieved by working with you. Share real-world examples of how you've helped clients overcome challenges, achieve their goals, and realize tangible benefits. By showcasing success stories and testimonials, you build credibility and trust with potential clients, increasing the likelihood of repeat business and referrals.

8. Continuously Improve and Innovate:

Continuous improvement and innovation are essential for staying ahead of the competition and delivering exceptional client experiences. Regularly assess your processes, practices, and service offerings to identify opportunities for improvement and innovation. Solicit feedback from clients and incorporate their input into your ongoing efforts to enhance the client experience. By continuously improving and innovating, you demonstrate your commitment to delivering value and exceeding client expectations, driving repeat business and referrals in the process.

In conclusion, leveraging positive client experiences for repeat business and referrals requires a strategic approach that prioritizes client satisfaction, delivers consistently high-quality service, exceeds expectations, builds strong relationships based on trust and respect, stays top of mind with regular follow-up, encourages and incentivizes referrals, showcases success stories and testimonials, and continuously improves and innovates. By implementing these strategies, service providers can maximize the value of positive client experiences, cultivate loyal clients, and generate a steady stream of referrals that fuel long-term growth and success. Through proactive and client-focused engagement, service providers can create a virtuous cycle of satisfaction, loyalty, and advocacy that drives sustainable business growth.

7. Resolving Conflict And Difficult Situations.

Chapter 7 of our book delves into the challenging yet inevitable aspect of resolving conflict and difficult situations in client-service provider relationships. Conflict and challenging scenarios can arise at any point during a project, testing the resilience and effectiveness of the partnership. In this chapter, we will explore strategies, techniques, and best practices for navigating conflict, addressing difficult situations, and finding constructive resolutions that preserve relationships and drive project success. Join us as we uncover practical insights and actionable approaches for managing conflict, fostering collaboration, and turning challenges into opportunities for growth and strengthened partnerships.

∧∧∧∧

i. Dealing With Confrontational Clients And Managing Challenging Conversations.

In the realm of client-service provider relationships, confrontational clients and challenging conversations are inevitable occurrences that require deft handling and strategic communication. These situations, although uncomfortable, present opportunities for building trust, resolving conflicts, and strengthening partnerships. In this section, we'll explore effective strategies for dealing with confrontational clients and managing challenging conversations with professionalism and poise.

1. Stay Calm and Composed:

When faced with a confrontational client or challenging conversation, it's crucial to maintain a calm and composed demeanor. Avoid reacting impulsively or defensively to provocation, as this can escalate tensions and hinder productive dialogue. Take a deep breath, center yourself, and approach the situation with a level head. By staying calm and composed, you project confidence and professionalism, setting the tone for a constructive exchange.

2. Listen Actively and Empathetically:

Active listening is a cornerstone of effective communication, particularly in challenging situations. Listen attentively to the client's concerns, grievances, and perspectives without interrupting or judging. Seek to understand the underlying emotions and motivations driving their behavior, and empathize with their perspective. Acknowledge their feelings and validate their experiences, demonstrating empathy and respect. By listening actively and empathetically, you foster trust and rapport, laying the groundwork for meaningful dialogue.

3. Acknowledge and Validate Concerns:

Validation is a powerful tool for defusing tension and de-escalating confrontational situations. Acknowledge the client's concerns, frustrations, and grievances, even if you disagree with their perspective. Validate their feelings and experiences, demonstrating understanding and empathy. Avoid dismissing or belittling their concerns, as this can exacerbate hostility and undermine trust. By acknowledging and validating the client's concerns, you show respect for their perspective and pave the way for constructive dialogue.

4. Communicate Clearly and Respectfully:

Effective communication is essential for navigating challenging conversations with confrontational clients. Be clear, concise, and respectful in your communication, avoiding ambiguity or ambiguity. Use neutral language and tone, focusing on facts and solutions rather than blame or judgment. Be mindful of your body language and nonverbal cues, as these can convey messages unintentionally. By communicating clearly and respectfully, you facilitate understanding and promote collaboration, even in difficult circumstances.

5. Set Boundaries and Maintain Professionalism:

While it's essential to empathize with the client and validate their concerns, it's equally important to set boundaries and maintain professionalism. Clearly communicate acceptable standards of behavior and expectations for the conversation, ensuring that all parties adhere to respectful and constructive communication norms. Firmly but diplomatically address any inappropriate behavior or language, redirecting the conversation back to productive dialogue. By setting boundaries and maintaining professionalism, you uphold the integrity of the interaction and foster a climate of mutual respect.

6. Focus on Solutions and Common Ground:

Rather than dwelling on the conflict or differences, focus the conversation on identifying solutions and common ground. Collaborate with the client to brainstorm potential resolutions that address their concerns while aligning with project objectives and constraints. Look for areas of agreement and shared interests, emphasizing the shared goal of achieving project success. By shifting the focus from the problem to the solution, you reframe the conversation in a positive light and encourage collaboration and compromise.

7. Follow Up and Document Agreements:

After the challenging conversation has concluded, follow up with the client to ensure clarity and reinforce agreements reached. Summarize key points of discussion, decisions made, and action items agreed upon in writing, and share this summary with the client for confirmation. Documenting agreements helps prevent misunderstandings and provides a record of the conversation for future reference. By following up and documenting agreements, you demonstrate accountability and commitment to honoring the resolution reached.

8. Learn and Grow from the Experience:

Every challenging conversation presents an opportunity for learning and growth. Take time to reflect on the interaction, considering what went well and areas for improvement. Seek feedback from colleagues or mentors to gain additional perspectives and insights. Use the experience as an opportunity to refine your communication skills, emotional intelligence, and conflict resolution abilities. By learning and growing from the experience, you become better equipped to handle similar situations in the future.

In conclusion, dealing with confrontational clients and managing challenging conversations requires a combination of emotional intelligence, communication skills, and professionalism. By staying calm and composed, listening actively and empathetically, acknowledging and validating concerns, communicating clearly and respectfully, setting boundaries and maintaining professionalism, focusing on solutions and common ground, following up and documenting agreements, and learning and growing from the experience, service providers can navigate confrontational situations with confidence and poise. Through effective conflict resolution and constructive dialogue, confrontational clients can be transformed into collaborative partners, fostering stronger relationships and driving mutual success.

∧∧∧∧

ii. Strategies For Addressing Disputes Over Budget And Scope.

Disputes over budget and scope are common challenges that arise in client-service provider relationships. These disputes can strain relationships, hinder project progress, and impact overall project outcomes. However, with proactive communication, strategic negotiation, and a focus on finding mutually beneficial solutions, these disputes can be effectively addressed. In this section, we'll explore practical strategies for resolving disputes over budget and scope and maintaining positive client relationships.

1. Establish Clear Expectations from the Outset:

Preventing disputes starts with setting clear expectations from the outset of the project. Clearly define the project scope, objectives, deliverables, timelines, and budget in the initial project agreement. Ensure that both parties have a shared understanding of the project scope and any potential limitations or constraints. By establishing clear expectations upfront, you minimize the risk of misunderstandings and disputes later on.

2. Communicate Proactively and Transparently:

Open and transparent communication is essential for addressing disputes over budget and scope effectively. Keep the client informed of any changes, challenges, or issues that may impact the project scope or budget as soon as they arise. Be proactive in communicating potential risks or deviations from the original plan, and work collaboratively with the client to identify solutions. Transparency builds trust and fosters a collaborative approach to resolving disputes.

3. Focus on Shared Goals and Objectives:

In the midst of a dispute, it's easy to lose sight of the shared goals and objectives that brought the client and service provider together in the first place. Reframe the conversation around these shared goals and objectives, emphasizing the mutual interests that both parties are working towards. By focusing on common ground, you can shift the focus from the dispute itself to finding solutions that benefit both parties.

4. Evaluate Options for Compromise:

When disputes arise, it's essential to explore options for compromise that address the concerns of both parties. Consider alternative solutions or adjustments to the project scope or budget that meet the client's needs while also aligning with the service provider's capabilities and constraints. Look for win-win solutions that allow both parties to achieve their objectives without compromising the integrity of the project.

5. Document Agreements and Changes:

Once a resolution has been reached, document the agreements and any changes to the project scope or budget in writing. Clearly outline the revised scope, timelines, deliverables, and budgetary considerations, and obtain the client's approval in writing. Documenting agreements helps prevent misunderstandings and provides a record of the resolution reached for future reference. By formalizing agreements in writing, you ensure clarity and accountability moving forward.

6. Seek Mediation or Third-Party Intervention:

In cases where disputes cannot be resolved through direct negotiation, consider seeking mediation or third-party intervention to facilitate resolution. A neutral mediator can help facilitate constructive dialogue between the client and service provider, identify underlying issues, and explore potential solutions. Third-party intervention can provide an objective perspective and help bridge communication gaps, leading to a more amicable resolution.

7. Learn from Disputes and Improve Processes:

Disputes over budget and scope provide valuable learning opportunities for improving processes and procedures moving forward. Take the time to reflect on the root causes of the dispute and identify areas for improvement in project management, communication, and client engagement. Incorporate lessons learned into your processes and practices to prevent similar disputes from arising in future projects. By continuously improving and refining your approach, you can mitigate the risk of disputes and strengthen client relationships over time.

8. Maintain Professionalism and Respect:

Throughout the dispute resolution process, it's essential to maintain professionalism and respect in all interactions with the client. Avoid engaging in personal attacks or hostile behavior, and focus on finding constructive solutions to the dispute. Treat the client with courtesy and respect, even if tensions are high, and strive to resolve the dispute in a manner that preserves the integrity of the relationship. By maintaining professionalism and respect, you demonstrate your commitment to resolving the dispute amicably and preserving the client-provider relationship.

In conclusion, addressing disputes over budget and scope requires proactive communication, strategic negotiation, and a focus on finding mutually beneficial solutions. By establishing clear expectations, communicating proactively and transparently, focusing on shared goals, evaluating options for compromise, documenting agreements, seeking mediation or third-party intervention, learning from disputes, improving processes, and maintaining professionalism and respect, service providers can effectively address disputes and preserve positive client relationships. Through proactive and collaborative dispute resolution, service providers can navigate challenges with confidence and preserve the integrity of client partnerships.

∧∧∧∧

iii. Knowing When To Escalate Issues And Seek Resolution.

In the dynamic landscape of client-service provider relationships, knowing when to escalate issues and seek resolution is a critical skill that can significantly impact project outcomes and client satisfaction. While many challenges can be resolved through direct communication and collaboration, there are instances where escalating issues to higher levels of authority or seeking external intervention is necessary to achieve a satisfactory resolution. In this section, we'll explore the indicators and best practices for knowing when to escalate issues and seek resolution effectively.

1. Exhaustion of Mitigation Measures:

One key indicator that it may be time to escalate an issue is the exhaustion of mitigation measures at the current level. If attempts to resolve the issue directly with the client or within the project team have been unsuccessful despite diligent efforts, escalating the issue to higher levels of authority may be necessary to explore alternative solutions or interventions. When mitigation measures have been exhausted, escalating the issue can help prevent further delays or escalation of the problem.

2. Impact on Project Progress or Deliverables:

Issues that have a significant impact on project progress or deliverables may warrant escalation to ensure timely resolution and mitigate potential risks. If an issue threatens to derail the project timeline, compromise the quality of deliverables, or exceed budgetary constraints, escalating the issue to relevant stakeholders or decision-makers becomes imperative to address the situation promptly and effectively. Timely escalation can help prevent further escalation of the issue and minimize the impact on project outcomes.

3. Violation of Contractual Agreements or Obligations:

Instances where the client or service provider is in violation of contractual agreements or obligations may necessitate escalation to ensure adherence to contractual terms and protect the interests of both parties. If attempts to resolve contractual disputes through direct negotiation have failed, escalating the issue to legal counsel or relevant authorities may be necessary to enforce contractual obligations or seek legal remedies. Escalating contractual disputes can help protect the rights and interests of both parties and facilitate a fair and equitable resolution.

4. Emergence of Ethical or Compliance Concerns:

Issues involving ethical or compliance concerns require careful consideration and may warrant escalation to ensure adherence to ethical standards and regulatory requirements. If an issue raises ethical dilemmas or compliance risks that cannot be resolved through internal channels, escalating the issue to regulatory bodies, industry associations, or legal authorities may be necessary to address the situation appropriately. Escalating ethical or compliance concerns demonstrates a commitment to upholding ethical standards and regulatory compliance, safeguarding the reputation and integrity of the organization.

5. Persistent Resistance or Unwillingness to Collaborate:

Persistent resistance or unwillingness to collaborate from the client or other stakeholders may indicate underlying issues that require escalation to facilitate resolution. If attempts to engage stakeholders in constructive dialogue or collaboration have been met with resistance or hostility, escalating the issue to higher levels of authority or seeking external intervention may be necessary to break through impasses and foster productive communication. Escalating issues involving persistent resistance demonstrates a commitment to resolving conflicts and promoting collaboration, even in challenging circumstances.

6. Escalation Protocols and Hierarchies:

Understanding the escalation protocols and hierarchies within the organization is essential for knowing when and how to escalate issues effectively. Establish clear escalation pathways and guidelines that outline when issues should be escalated, to whom, and under what circumstances. Ensure that team members are familiar with escalation protocols and empowered to escalate issues when necessary, without fear of reprisal or retaliation. By following established escalation protocols, you can ensure that issues are addressed promptly and efficiently, minimizing disruptions to project progress.

7. Evaluation of Risks and Impacts:

Before escalating an issue, it's essential to evaluate the potential risks and impacts associated with escalation carefully. Consider the potential consequences of escalating the issue, including impacts on project timelines, budgets, client relationships, and organizational reputation. Weigh the benefits and drawbacks of escalation against the likelihood of achieving a satisfactory resolution through other means. By conducting a thorough risk assessment, you can make informed decisions about whether escalation is warranted in a given situation.

8. Seek Guidance and Support:

When in doubt about whether to escalate an issue, seek guidance and support from relevant stakeholders, mentors, or colleagues. Discuss the situation with trusted advisors or individuals who have experience navigating similar challenges. Solicit input and perspectives from diverse sources to gain a comprehensive understanding of the issue and potential courses of action. By seeking guidance and support, you can make informed decisions about whether escalation is the appropriate course of action and how best to proceed.

In conclusion, knowing when to escalate issues and seek resolution requires careful consideration of various factors, including exhaustion of mitigation measures, impact on project progress or deliverables, violation of contractual agreements or obligations, emergence of ethical or compliance concerns, persistent resistance or unwillingness to collaborate, escalation protocols and hierarchies, evaluation of risks and impacts, and seeking guidance and support. By recognizing the indicators for escalation and following established escalation protocols, service providers can effectively address issues and disputes, safeguard project outcomes, and maintain positive client relationships. Through proactive and strategic escalation, service providers can navigate challenges with confidence and ensure the timely resolution of issues, ultimately contributing to project success and client satisfaction.

8. Learning And Growing From Experiences.

Chapter 8 of our book is dedicated to the invaluable process of learning and growing from experiences encountered in client-service provider relationships. In this chapter, we'll explore the importance of reflecting on past experiences, both successes, and challenges, and extracting valuable insights that contribute to personal and professional growth. By embracing a mindset of continuous learning and improvement, service providers can leverage their experiences to refine their skills, enhance their capabilities, and deliver even greater value to clients in the future. Join us as we delve into practical strategies, reflective exercises, and actionable takeaways for leveraging experiences as catalysts for growth and success.

∧∧∧∧

i. Reflecting On Past Experiences With Clients And Budget Negotiations.

———

Reflecting on past experiences with clients and budget negotiations is a powerful tool for personal and professional growth in the realm of client-service provider relationships. By examining both successes and challenges encountered in past engagements, service providers can gain valuable insights, identify areas for improvement, and refine their approach to budget negotiations. In this section, we'll explore the benefits of reflecting on past experiences with clients and budget negotiations and provide practical strategies for leveraging these reflections to enhance future performance.

1. Extracting Lessons Learned:

Reflecting on past experiences with clients and budget negotiations allows service providers to extract valuable lessons learned from each engagement. Take the time to analyze past projects and budget negotiations, identifying what went well and areas for improvement. Consider factors such as communication strategies, negotiation techniques, client expectations, and project outcomes. By extracting lessons learned from past experiences, service providers can gain valuable insights that inform future decision-making and behavior.

2. Identifying Patterns and Trends:

Examining past experiences with clients and budget negotiations can help service providers identify patterns and trends that may impact future engagements. Look for recurring themes or issues that have emerged in past projects, such as common challenges, client preferences, or successful negotiation strategies. By identifying patterns and trends, service providers can anticipate potential challenges and proactively develop strategies to address them in future engagements.

3. Recognizing Successes and Achievements:

Reflecting on past experiences with clients and budget negotiations provides an opportunity to recognize successes and achievements achieved in previous engagements. Celebrate milestones, accomplishments, and positive outcomes from past projects, acknowledging the hard work and dedication that contributed to their success. Recognizing successes boosts morale, instills confidence, and motivates service providers to continue delivering excellence in future engagements.

4. Evaluating Communication and Relationship Dynamics:

Communication and relationship dynamics play a critical role in client-service provider relationships and budget negotiations. Reflect on past interactions with clients, assessing the effectiveness of communication strategies and relationship dynamics. Consider factors such as clarity of communication, responsiveness, trust, and rapport with clients. Evaluate what communication strategies were successful and which ones could be improved upon in future engagements.

5. Assessing Negotiation Strategies and Outcomes:

Budget negotiations are a fundamental aspect of client-service provider relationships, requiring skillful negotiation and compromise. Reflect on past budget negotiations, assessing the effectiveness of negotiation strategies and outcomes achieved. Consider factors such as preparation, flexibility, assertiveness, and the ability to find mutually beneficial solutions. Evaluate what negotiation strategies were successful in achieving desired outcomes and areas for improvement in future negotiations.

6. Soliciting Feedback from Clients:

Feedback from clients is a valuable source of insight for reflecting on past experiences and improving future performance. Solicit feedback from clients after project completion, asking for their honest assessment of the engagement, including communication, service quality, and budget negotiations. Use client feedback to identify areas of strength and opportunities for improvement, incorporating their input into future engagements. By actively seeking feedback from clients, service providers demonstrate a commitment to continuous improvement and client satisfaction.

7. Setting Goals for Improvement:

Based on reflections on past experiences with clients and budget negotiations, set goals for improvement in future engagements. Identify specific areas where you aim to enhance your skills, refine your approach, or achieve better outcomes. Establish measurable goals that align with your professional development objectives and track progress over time. By setting goals for improvement, service providers create a roadmap for growth and development that drives continuous improvement in client engagements.

8. Implementing Changes and Adjustments:

Finally, leverage reflections on past experiences to implement changes and adjustments that enhance future performance. Based on lessons learned, patterns identified, and goals set for improvement, make proactive changes to your approach, processes, or strategies. Incorporate feedback from clients and insights gained from past experiences into your decision-making and behavior. By implementing changes and adjustments, service providers demonstrate a commitment to learning and growth, driving continuous improvement in client engagements.

In conclusion, reflecting on past experiences with clients and budget negotiations is a valuable process for personal and professional growth in client-service provider relationships. By extracting lessons learned, identifying patterns and trends, recognizing successes and achievements, evaluating communication and relationship dynamics, assessing negotiation strategies and outcomes, soliciting feedback from clients, setting goals for improvement, and implementing changes and adjustments, service providers can leverage past experiences to enhance future performance. Through reflection and continuous improvement, service providers can deliver greater value to clients, strengthen relationships, and achieve long-term success in client engagements.

∧∧∧∧

ii. Identifying Lessons Learned And Areas For Improvement.

Identifying lessons learned and areas for improvement is a critical aspect of personal and professional growth in client-service provider relationships. By reflecting on past experiences, both successes and challenges, service providers can extract valuable insights, identify patterns, and develop strategies for enhancing their performance in future engagements. In this section, we'll explore the importance of identifying lessons learned and areas for improvement and provide practical strategies for leveraging these insights to drive continuous growth and development.

1. Reflecting on Past Experiences:

The first step in identifying lessons learned and areas for improvement is to reflect on past experiences with clients and projects. Take the time to review past engagements, assessing what went well and areas where challenges were encountered. Reflect on the communication dynamics, project management processes, client interactions, and outcomes achieved. By reflecting on past experiences, service providers can gain valuable insights into their strengths, weaknesses, and opportunities for growth.

2. Analyzing Successes and Challenges:

Once past experiences have been reviewed, it's essential to analyze both successes and challenges encountered in client engagements. Identify specific instances where objectives were successfully achieved, milestones were met, or positive outcomes were realized. Likewise, analyze instances where challenges were encountered, such as budget overruns, communication breakdowns, or scope creep. By analyzing successes and challenges, service providers can identify patterns and trends that inform areas for improvement.

3. Seeking Feedback and Input:

Feedback from clients, colleagues, and other stakeholders is a valuable source of insight for identifying lessons learned and areas for improvement. Solicit feedback from clients after project completion, asking for their honest assessment of the engagement, including communication, service quality, and outcomes achieved. Additionally, seek input from colleagues and peers who may have observed your performance or have insights to share. By seeking feedback and input, service providers gain diverse perspectives that inform their self-assessment.

4. Identifying Strengths and Weaknesses:

Based on reflections and feedback received, identify your strengths and weaknesses as a service provider. Acknowledge areas where you excel, such as effective communication skills, technical expertise, or problem-solving abilities. Similarly, recognize areas where improvement is needed, such as time management, negotiation skills, or client relationship management. By identifying strengths and weaknesses, service providers can focus their efforts on leveraging strengths and addressing weaknesses.

5. Recognizing Opportunities for Growth:

In addition to identifying weaknesses, it's essential to recognize opportunities for growth and development. Consider areas where you have the potential to improve your skills, expand your knowledge, or broaden your expertise. Look for opportunities to take on new challenges, pursue professional development opportunities, or acquire additional training or certifications. By recognizing opportunities for growth, service providers can take proactive steps to enhance their capabilities and performance.

6. Setting SMART Goals:

Based on the insights gained from reflection and analysis, set SMART (Specific, Measurable, Achievable, Relevant, Time-bound) goals for improvement. Identify specific areas where you aim to enhance your performance or develop new skills. Ensure that goals are measurable and achievable within a realistic timeframe. By setting SMART goals, service providers create a roadmap for growth and development that guides their actions and progress.

7. Developing Action Plans:

Once goals have been established, develop action plans outlining the steps needed to achieve them. Break down goals into smaller, manageable tasks and identify resources, support, and timelines for completion. Consider what actions are needed to address weaknesses, capitalize on strengths, and pursue opportunities for growth. By developing action plans, service providers create a structured approach to achieving their goals and driving continuous improvement.

8. Implementing Continuous Improvement Practices:

Finally, embrace a mindset of continuous improvement and incorporate practices that support ongoing growth and development. Regularly review progress towards goals, adjust action plans as needed, and celebrate achievements along the way. Seek out opportunities for feedback, learning, and skill-building, both within and outside of client engagements. By embracing continuous improvement practices, service providers demonstrate a commitment to excellence and lifelong learning.

In conclusion, identifying lessons learned and areas for improvement is essential for personal and professional growth in client-service provider relationships. By reflecting on past experiences, analyzing successes and challenges, seeking feedback and input, identifying strengths and weaknesses, recognizing opportunities for growth, setting SMART goals, developing action plans, and implementing continuous improvement practices, service providers can drive continuous growth and development. Through self-awareness, proactive goal-setting, and a commitment to lifelong learning, service providers can enhance their capabilities, deliver greater value to clients, and achieve long-term success in their careers.

^^^^

iii. Developing A Proactive Approach To Managing Client Expectations In The Future.

In the dynamic landscape of client-service provider relationships, managing client expectations is paramount to project success and client satisfaction. Developing a proactive approach to managing client expectations involves anticipating needs, fostering clear communication, and building trust throughout the engagement. In this section, we'll explore practical strategies for proactively managing client expectations in the future, ensuring alignment, transparency, and mutual understanding from project inception to completion.

1. Establish Clear Communication Channels:

One of the cornerstones of a proactive approach to managing client expectations is establishing clear communication channels from the outset of the engagement. Foster open lines of communication with clients, providing multiple channels for interaction, such as email, phone calls, and project management platforms. Clearly communicate expectations regarding communication frequency, response times, and escalation procedures to ensure that clients feel informed and supported throughout the engagement.

2. Define Project Scope and Objectives Clearly:

Clearly defining project scope and objectives is essential for managing client expectations and avoiding scope creep. Work collaboratively with clients to establish a detailed project scope document that outlines deliverables, timelines, milestones, and success criteria. Clearly communicate any limitations or constraints that may impact project scope, such as budgetary constraints or resource availability. By defining project scope and objectives clearly, you set the foundation for a successful engagement and mitigate the risk of misunderstandings or discrepancies later on.

3. Set Realistic Expectations from the Onset:

Managing client expectations begins with setting realistic expectations from the onset of the engagement. Be transparent with clients about what can realistically be achieved within the project constraints, including timelines, budgets, and resource availability. Avoid overpromising or making commitments that cannot be fulfilled, as this can lead to disappointment and dissatisfaction. By setting realistic expectations upfront, you establish trust and credibility with clients and foster a collaborative approach to project delivery.

4. Provide Regular Progress Updates:

Keeping clients informed of project progress is essential for managing expectations and building trust throughout the engagement. Provide regular progress updates, sharing insights into project milestones, achievements, and challenges encountered. Be proactive in communicating any deviations from the original plan, such as delays or unforeseen obstacles, and work collaboratively with clients to address them. Regular progress updates demonstrate transparency, accountability, and a commitment to keeping clients informed every step of the way.

5. Anticipate and Address Potential Issues Proactively:

A proactive approach to managing client expectations involves anticipating and addressing potential issues before they escalate. Anticipate potential challenges or concerns that may arise during the course of the engagement and develop contingency plans to address them proactively. Communicate any anticipated risks or obstacles to clients, along with proposed solutions or mitigation strategies. By addressing potential issues proactively, you demonstrate foresight and proactive problem-solving, earning clients' confidence and trust.

6. Foster Collaborative Decision-Making:

Involve clients in the decision-making process throughout the engagement to ensure alignment and foster collaboration. Seek client input and feedback on key decisions, such as project milestones, deliverables, and resource allocation. Encourage open dialogue and constructive feedback, creating a collaborative environment where clients feel valued and empowered. By fostering collaborative decision-making, you build stronger relationships with clients and ensure that project outcomes meet their expectations.

7. Manage Change Effectively:

Change is inevitable in client-service provider relationships, and managing change effectively is essential for maintaining alignment and managing expectations. Develop a change management process that outlines how changes to project scope, timelines, or budgets will be evaluated, communicated, and implemented. Clearly communicate the impact of proposed changes on project objectives and constraints, and work collaboratively with clients to assess trade-offs and make informed decisions. By managing change effectively, you minimize disruptions to project progress and ensure that client expectations are managed appropriately.

8. Conduct Post-Project Reviews and Feedback Sessions:

After project completion, conduct post-project reviews and feedback sessions with clients to gather insights and assess satisfaction levels. Solicit feedback on all aspects of the engagement, including communication, service quality, and outcomes achieved. Use feedback received to identify areas for improvement and inform future engagements. Post-project reviews demonstrate a commitment to continuous improvement and client satisfaction, reinforcing trust and credibility with clients.

In conclusion, developing a proactive approach to managing client expectations involves establishing clear communication channels, defining project scope and objectives clearly, setting realistic expectations from the onset, providing regular progress updates, anticipating and addressing potential issues proactively, fostering collaborative decision-making, managing change effectively, and conducting post-project reviews and feedback sessions. By proactively managing client expectations, service providers can build trust, foster collaboration, and ensure successful project outcomes that meet or exceed client expectations. Through transparent communication, proactive problem-solving, and a commitment to continuous improvement, service providers can cultivate long-term partnerships built on mutual respect and shared success.

9. Conclusion.

IN THE REALM OF ENTREPRENEURSHIP, mastering the art of navigating unrealistic budget expectations is a crucial skill that can make or break the success of ventures. Throughout this comprehensive guide, titled "Navigating Unrealistic Budget Expectations: A Guide for New Entrepreneurs," we've embarked on a journey to equip aspiring entrepreneurs with the knowledge, strategies, and insights needed to navigate the complexities of budget negotiations and client relationships successfully.

From defining unrealistic budget expectations to developing proactive approaches for managing client expectations, each chapter has offered practical guidance and actionable advice tailored to the unique challenges faced by new entrepreneurs. As we bring this book to a close, let's reflect on some key insights and takeaways:

1. Understanding Unrealistic Budget Expectations: We began by exploring the nuances of unrealistic budget expectations, defining what constitutes an unrealistic budget and understanding the underlying psychology behind clients' budget expectations. By recognizing the factors that contribute to unrealistic budget demands, entrepreneurs can better navigate negotiations and set realistic expectations.

2. Impact on Business Operations and Profitability: Unrealistic budget expectations can have significant implications for business operations and profitability. We examined how such expectations can strain resources, compromise quality, and erode profitability, underscoring the importance of managing client expectations effectively to protect the bottom line.

3. Strategies for Effective Communication: Clear and transparent communication is essential for managing client expectations and negotiating budgets successfully. We explored techniques for articulating budget constraints, establishing open channels for dialogue and feedback, and educating clients about industry standards and typical costs. By fostering open communication and collaboration, entrepreneurs can build trust and alignment with clients.

<u>4. Aligning Expectations with Budget Limitations:</u> Strategies for aligning client expectations with budget limitations are crucial for maintaining profitability and delivering value to clients. We discussed techniques for identifying areas for negotiation and compromise, presenting alternative solutions within budget constraints, and maintaining professionalism and assertiveness during negotiations. By navigating negotiations strategically, entrepreneurs can achieve mutually beneficial outcomes.

<u>5. Managing Scope Creep:</u> Scope creep poses a significant challenge in client engagements and can derail projects if left unchecked. We explored strategies for recognizing signs of scope creep, implementing preventive measures, and communicating changes in scope effectively to clients. By managing scope creep proactively, entrepreneurs can minimize disruptions and deliver projects on time and within budget.

As we conclude this guide, let's remember that navigating unrealistic budget expectations is not a one-time task but an ongoing process that requires diligence, communication, and adaptability. By embracing the principles and strategies outlined in this book, new entrepreneurs can navigate budget negotiations with confidence, protect their profitability, and build lasting relationships with clients.

Thank you for joining us on this journey through the complexities of budget negotiations and client relationships. May the insights and strategies shared in this guide empower you to overcome challenges, seize opportunities, and achieve success in your entrepreneurial endeavors. Here's to navigating unrealistic budget expectations with resilience, wisdom, and determination.

Also by Priscilla Rogers

Living Right - Moral Stories For A Beautiful Life
Living Right - 50 Stories Of Moral Clarity - Book 1
Living Right - 50 Stories Of Moral Clarity - Book 2
Living Right - 50 Stories Of Moral Clarity - Book 3

Standalone
Christmas Stories of Joy - 50 Short Stories
Flash of Fantasy - 50 Magical Adventures
Flashback: 50 Stories of Nostalgia
Love In A Flash - 50 Romantic Short Stories
Uptown, Downtown, All Around: New York Short Stories.
Stoicism Unbound: Navigating the Modern World with Ancient Wisdom
Sweet Dreams Delight: 30 Bedtime Short Stories
Navigating Unrealistic Budget Expectations: A Guide for New Entrepreneurs

Also by Ishan Khan

Flash Frights: 50 Terrifying Tales of Horror
Flash of Fantasy - 50 Magical Adventures
Flashback: 50 Stories of Nostalgia
Sci-Fi Snapshots: 50 Quick Trips To The Future
Whispers In The Dark - 50 Short Thriller Stories
Uptown, Downtown, All Around: New York Short Stories.
Mumbai: City of Dreams, Stories of Reality.
Secrets And Shadows: 25 Short Thriller Stories.
Navigating Unrealistic Budget Expectations: A Guide for New Entrepreneurs

www.ingramcontent.com/pod-product-compliance
Lightning Source LLC
Chambersburg PA
CBHW050549160726
48003CB00002B/815